Government Support to Agricultural Insurance

Government Support to Agricultural Insurance
Challenges and Options
for Developing Countries

Olivier Mahul
and
Charles J. Stutley

THE WORLD BANK
Washington, D.C.

Cover photos: Image99/Jupiter images
Cover design: Naylor Design, Inc.

ISBN: 978-0-8213-8217-2
eISBN: 978-0-8213-8219-6
DOI: 10.1596/978-0-8213-8217-2

Library of Congress Cataloging-in-Publication Data has been applied for.

Contents

Tables

Foreword

Agriculture remains a source of livelihood for almost half of humanity. It is also a source of growth for national economies and can be a provider of investment opportunities for the private sector. However, millions of poor people face prospects of tragic crop failure or livestock mortality when, as a result of climate change, rainfall patterns shift or extreme events such as drought and floods become more frequent. Agricultural insurance is key in assisting farmers, herders, and governments lessen the negative financial impact of these adverse natural events.

This book is the result of 10 years of involvement in agricultural insurance by the Insurance for the Poor team, Non-Bank Financial Institutions unit in the Global Capital Markets Development Department of the World Bank's Financial and Private Sector Development (FPD) Vice Presidency. Working together with our World Bank regional colleagues, our team has assisted countries in developing sustainable agricultural insurance programs in more than 20 countries. Noteworthy examples are the weather-based crop insurance scheme in India, in which more than one million farmers are currently insured; and the index-based livestock insurance program in Mongolia, where more than 600,000 animals are covered against adverse weather.

Based on a unique review of agricultural insurance programs in 65 advanced and emerging countries, this book pulls together collective knowledge and experiences to help policy makers promote sound agricultural insurance programs. It provides policy makers with a current picture of the spectrum of institutional frameworks and experiences with agricultural insurance, ranging from countries in which the public sector provides no support to those in which governments heavily subsidize agricultural insurance.

This book makes a compelling case for public-private partnerships in the promotion of agricultural insurance, supported by the donor community and international financial institutions like the World Bank. It provides a systemic approach to making agricultural insurance markets more stable, efficient, and accessible.

I hope that this book will further contribute to the dialogue on agricultural risk management, highlighting the need for countries to strengthen their policy and institutional frameworks to support agricultural insurance, and also assisting governments in meeting the ensuing challenges.

Janamitra Devan
Vice President
Financial and Private Sector Development Network
World Bank/International Finance Corporation

Acknowledgments

The co-authors of this book are Olivier Mahul (Insurance for the Poor Program Coordinator, Non-Bank Financial Institutions unit in the Global Capital Markets Development Department [GCMNB], World Bank) and Charles Stutley (International Agricultural Insurance Consultant, GCMNB, World Bank).

This book is based on a World Bank survey of agricultural insurance markets conducted in 2008 under the leadership of Olivier Mahul and Charles Stutley. The team also comprised William Dick (consultant, Commodity Risk Management Group, Agricultural and Rural Development, World Bank), Barry Goodwin (Professor of Agricultural Economics, North Carolina State University), Ramiro Iturrioz (Senior Agricultural Insurance Specialist, GCMNB, World Bank); Roman Shynkarenko (consultant, GCMNB, World Bank), and Ligia Vado (consultant, GCMNB, World Bank). The team owes thanks to Sevara Atamuratova, Uloaku Echebiri, Ernst Lutz, and Tina Lutz for their editorial contributions and technical work.

The authors are grateful to the peer reviewers, Brian Wright (University of California at Berkeley), Peter Hazell (Consultative Group on International Agricultural Research), and Don Larson (Development Research Group, World Bank). The team also thanks Loic Chiquier (Manager, GCMNB) and Steven Jaffee (Commodity Risk Management Group, Agricultural and Rural Development, World Bank) for their comments.

The authors sincerely thank the many respondents who kindly completed the questionnaire sent to them as part of the World Bank Survey on agricultural insurance in 2008, or who separately provided country information. They are listed below.

Agria Djurförsäkring (Sweden)
Agriculture Financial Services
   Corporation (Alberta, Canada)
Agricultural Insurance Fund
   (A.P.I.F.) (Iran)
Agriculture Insurance Company
   of India Ltd. (AICI) (India)
Agriculture Insurance Consultant
   (China)
Agricultural Insurance Pool
   (TARSIM) (Turkey)
Agroasemex, S.A. (Mexico)
Agrodosa (Dominican Republic)
Agroseguro, S.A. (Spain)
Aon Re (Argentina)
Aon Re (Australia)
Aon Re (New Zealand)
Aon Re (South Africa)
Aseguradora Magallanes (Chile)
Asiban SA (Romania)
Banco de Seguros del Estado del
   (Uruguay)
CA Seguros, S.A. (Portugal)
Cámara Hondureña de Asegu-
   radores (Honduras)
CGM Gallagher Group (Jamaica)
Concordia Polska TUW (Poland)
Ethiopian Insurance Corporation
   (Ethiopia)
Federal Agency of State Support
   of Insurance in Agroindustrial
   Production (Russia)

GlobalAgRisk (United States)
Hannover Re (Germany)
Index Based Livestock Insurance
   Project Implementation Unit
   (Mongolia)
Instituto Nacional de Seguros
   (Costa Rica)
Instituto Nicaragüense de Seguros
   y Reaseguros (Nicaragua)
Ismea (Italy)
Kanat (Israel)
League of Insurance Organiza-
   tions of Ukraine (Ukraine)
Mapfre Colombia (Colombia)
Mclarens Toplis Peru S.A. (Peru)
Ministère de l'Alimentation, de
   l'Agriculture et de la Pêche
   (France)
Ministerio de Ganadería, Agricul-
   tura y Pesca (MGAP) (Uruguay)
Ministry of Finance (Azerbaijan)
Moldasig (Republic of Moldova)
Munich Re (Argentina)
Nico General Insurance Company
   Limited (Malawi)
Nigerian Agricultural Insurance
   Corporation (Nigeria)
North Carolina State University
   (United States)
Nyala Insurance S.C. (Ethiopia)
Office of the Insurance Commis-
   sion (Thailand)

Oficina de Riesgo Agropecuario (Argentina)

OTP Garancia Insurance Ltd. Co. (Hungary)

Paris Re (France)

Partner Re (Chile)

Philippine Crop Insurance Corporation (The Philippines)

Schweizer Hagel (Switzerland)

Seguros Colonial (Ecuador)

Shiekan Insurance & Reinsurance Co. Ltd. (Sudan)

Siam Commercial Samaggi Insurance Public Company Limited (Thailand)

Société Centrale de Réassurance (Morocco)

State Agency for Regulation of Finance Market and Finance Institutions (Kazakhstan)

Swiss Re (Brazil)

Swiss Re (Switzerland)

Swiss Re America Corporation (United States)

TAGH Gestión (Argentina)

Thai Re Insurance Public Co., Ltd. (Thailand)

Windward Islands Crop Insurance Ltd. (Dominica)

Abbreviations

Agroseguro	Agrupación Española de Entidaded Aseguradores de los Seguros Agrarios Cominados, S.A. (Spanish Pool of Insurers of the Combined Agricultural Insurance Program)
AICI	Agricultural Insurance Company of India
A&O	administration and operating
EU	European Union
FAO	Food and Agriculture Organization
FCIP	Federal Crop Insurance Program
GDP	gross domestic product
GNI	gross national income
INS	Instituto Nacional de Seguros (Costa Rican public insurance company)
LIIP	Livestock Indemnity Insurance Pool
MPCI	multiple peril crop insurance
NAIS	National Agricultural Insurance Scheme
NASFAM	National Association of Small Farmers
NDVI	normalized dry vegetative index
PCIC	Philippines Crop Insurance Corporation
PPP	public-private partnership
PRONAF	Programa Nacional de Fortalecimento da Agricultura Familiar (National Program for the Strengthening of Family Agriculture)
R&D	research and development

SEAF	Seguro da Agricultura Familiar (Brazilian Insurance for Family Agriculture)
SIPAC	System for the Protection of Climatic Risks
UNCTAD	United Nations Conference on Trade and Development
WTO	World Trade Organization

Glossary

Accumulation   Concentration of similar risks in a particular area such that an insured event may result in several losses at the same time.

Actuarial   Branch of statistics dealing with the probability of an event occurring. Accurate actuarial calculations require basic data over a sufficient time period to permit the likelihood of future events to be predicted with a degree of certainty.

Ad Hoc Response   Relief arranged in the aftermath of a disaster. Ad hoc responses are generally less efficient than planned responses or a well-designed risk management framework.

Adverse Selection   Situation in which potential insurance purchasers know more about their risks than the insurer does, leading to participation by high-risk individuals and nonparticipation by low-risk individuals. Insurers react by charging higher premiums or not insuring at all.

Agricultural Insurance   Insurance applied to crops, livestock, aquaculture, and forestry. Buildings and equipment are not usually covered by agricultural insurance, although they may be insured by the same insurer under a different policy.

Area-based Index Insurance   Insurance contracts written against specific perils or events defined and recorded at a regional level (county or district in the case of yields, local weather station in the case of insured weather events). Indemnities are paid based on losses at the regional rather than farm level.

Asset Risk   Risk of damage to or theft of production equipment or other assets.

Asymmetric Information   Information imbalance that occurs when one party to a transaction possesses more or better information than the other. Buyers of insurance products typically have better information about their level of risk exposure, which they may hide from insurers in order to obtain lower premium rates.

Basis Risk   Risk that index measurements will not match individual losses. As the geographical area covered by the index increases, basis risk increases as well.

Capacity   Maximum amount of insurance or reinsurance that an insurer, reinsurer, or insurance market will accept.

Catastrophe   Severe, usually sudden, disaster that results in heavy losses.

Ceding Company   Direct insurer that places all or part of an original risk on a reinsurer.

Claim   An insurer's application for indemnity payment after a covered loss occurs.

Cognitive Failure   Failure of decision makers to correctly assess the possibility of infrequent catastrophic risks.

Coinsurance   1. Situation in which the insured is liable for part of every loss, often expressed as a percentage of the sum insured. 2. Situation in which each of several insurers covers part of a risk.

Collective Policy   Policy issued on behalf of a number of insurers or covering a number of items, each insured separately.

Combined Loss Ratio   Proportion of claims paid (or payable) plus administrative and operating expenses (A&O) to premiums earned. A combined loss ratio greater than 1 (or 100 percent) indicates that the premiums collected from the insured are not sufficient to pay the claim (indemnity) and cover A&O expenses (that is, the insurer faces an underwriting loss).

Commission   Proportion of the premium paid by the insurer to the agent for procuring and serving the policyholder.

Correlated Risks   Risks that are likely to affect many individuals or households at the same time. For example, coffee growers in the same community are likely to be simultaneously affected by a decrease in the price of coffee. Futures and options markets can be used to transfer these risks to parties outside the local community.

Country Risk Profile   Level of risk exposure of a country, determined by the occurrence of events such as price shocks and adverse weather events that affect major private and public assets and economic activities within a country at the micro, meso, and macro levels.

Crop Insurance   Insurance that provides financial compensation for production or revenue losses resulting from specified or multiple perils, such as hail, windstorm, fire, or flood. Most crop insurance pays for the loss of physical production or yield. Coverage is also often available for loss of the productive asset, such as trees in the case of fruit crops.

Deductible   Amount of a claim the insured has to bear, expressed as a percentage of the sum insured or as a fixed amount.

Default   Failure to fulfill the obligations of a contract.

Direct Premium Subsidy   Subsidy calculated as a percentage of the insurance premium paid. Such a subsidy is problematic because it disproportionately benefits high-risk farmers who pay higher premiums. Attracting higher-risk farmers can significantly increase the costs of insurance.

Disaster-index Insurance   Insurance contract in which payments are triggered by extreme weather events. Disaster-index insurance is a form of weather insurance. See also *Index insurance* and *weather index insurance.*

Ex Ante Risk Mechanism   Risk management action taken before a potential risk event occurs.

Excess-of-loss   Form of reinsurance under which recoveries are due when given loss exceeds ceding company's retention defined in agreement.

Ex Post Risk Mechanism   Risk management action developed in reaction to an event.

Exposure   Amount (sum insured) exposed to insured perils at any one time. In crop insurance, exposure may increase and then decrease during the coverage period, following the growth stages of the crop from planting to harvest.

Fondos   Nonprofit civil associations in Mexico that pool crop yield risks among farmers with similar risk profiles.

Gross Net Premium Income   Gross written premium of a primary insurer minus cancellations, refunds, and reinsurance premium paid to other reinsurers. See also *Original gross premium* and *producer premium.*

Hazard   Physical or moral feature that increases the potential for a loss arising from an insured peril or the degree of damage.

High-probability Low-consequence Events   Frequent risks that cause mild to moderate damage. Insurance products are seldom offered for such events, because the transactions costs associated with them make the insurance cost prohibitive for most potential purchasers. The high transactions costs partly reflect information asymmetries that cause moral hazard and adverse selection. See also *Adverse selection* and *moral hazard.*

Indemnity   Amount the insurer pays the insured, in the form of cash, repair, replacement, or reinstatement, in the event of an insured loss. The indemnity cannot exceed the actual value of the asset insured just before the loss. For many crops, an escalating indemnity level is often established as the growing season progresses.

Independent Risks   Risks—such as the risks of automobile accidents, fire, or illness—that generally occur independently across households. Such statistical independence allows effective risk pooling across entities in the same insurance pool, making insurance possible. For independent risks, the law of large numbers suggests that, on average, the insurance indemnity paid to claimants in a particular year can be offset by the premiums received from clients who did not incur indemnifiable losses. See also *Risk pooling.*

Index Insurance   Insurance that makes indemnity payments based not on an assessment of the policyholder's individual loss but rather on measures of an index that is assumed to proxy actual losses. See also *Area-based index insurance* and *weather-index insurance*.

Informational Constraint   Constraint imposed by limited access to or availability of reliable data.

Institutional Risk   Risk generated by unexpected changes in regulations, especially in import and export regimes, that affect producers' activities and profits.

Insurability   Conditions that determine the viability of insurance as a method of managing a particular risk.

Insurable Interest   Interest that exists when an insured derives a financial benefit from the continuous existence of the insured object or suffers a financial loss from the loss of the insured object.

Insurance   Financial mechanism that aims to reduce the uncertainty of loss by pooling a large number of uncertainties so that the burden of loss is distributed. Generally, each policyholder pays a contribution to a fund in the form of a premium, commensurate with the risk he or she introduces. The insurer uses these funds to pay the losses (indemnities) suffered by any insured.

Insurance Agent   Person who solicits, negotiates, or implements insurance contracts on behalf of the insurer.

Insurance Broker   Person who represents the insured in finding an insurer or insurers for a risk and negotiating the terms of the insurance contract. A broker may also act as an agent (for the insurer) for the purposes of delivering a policy to and collecting premiums from the insured.

Insurance Policy   Formal document (including all clauses, riders, and endorsements) that expresses the terms, exceptions, and conditions of the contract of insurance between the insurer and the insured.

Insured Peril   Cause of loss stated in the policy, which on its occurrence entitles the insured to make a claim.

Layer   Range of potential loss covered by insurance. See also *Risk layering*.

Loss Adjustment   Determination of the extent of damage resulting from occurrence of an insured peril and the settlement of the claim.

Loss Ratio   Proportion of claims paid (or payable) to premiums earned, usually expressed as the total gross claim or indemnity divided by the total or original gross premium, expressed as a ratio or percentage. A loss ratio greater than 1 (or 100 percent) indicates that the amount of the claim (indemnity) paid by the insurer exceeds the amount of the premiums collected from the insured (inclusive of premium subsidy). See also *Producer loss ratio*.

Low-probability High-consequence Events   Events that occur infrequently but cause substantial damage. Decision makers, including agricultural producers, tend to underestimate their exposure to such events, because they forget the severity of the loss experienced during infrequent extreme weather events. For this reason, an insurance product that protects against these losses is frequently discounted or ignored by producers trying to determine the value of an insurance contract. See also *Cognitive failure.*

Market Failure   Inability of a market to provide certain goods at the optimal level because market prices are not equal to the social opportunity costs of resources. The high cost of financing catastrophic disaster risk prohibits most private insurance companies from covering this risk, resulting in market failure.

Moral Hazard   Problems generated when the insured's behavior can influence the extent of damage that qualifies for insurance payouts. Examples of moral hazard are carelessness and irresponsibility.

Nonproportional Treaty Reinsurance   Agreement in which the reinsurer agrees to pay all losses that exceed a specified limit arising from an insured portfolio of business. The limit, which is set by the reinsurer, may be monetary (for example, excess of loss) or a percentage of original gross premiums (for example, stop loss). The rates charged by the reinsurer are calculated independently of the original rates for the insurance charged to the insured.

Original Gross Premium   Amount payable by the insured to the original insurer, including the technical premium, to cover expected losses and catastrophe losses plus commercial loadings to cover marketing and acquisition costs, administration and operating expenses, and profit margin.

Premium   Monetary sum payable by the insured to the insurers for the period (or term) of insurance granted by the policy; the premium rate x the amount of the insurance; the cost of an option contract paid by the buyer to the seller. See also *Original gross premium.*

Premium Rate   Price per unit of insurance, normally expressed as a percentage of the sum insured.

Premium Subsidy   Amount of the total premium paid by the government or a third party.

Producer Loss Ratio   Proportion of claims paid (or payable) by the insured that is net of the premium subsidy paid by the government.

Producer Premium   Amount of the total premium paid by the insured following deduction of the subsidized proportion of premium.

Probable Maximum Loss   Largest loss believed possible for a certain type of business in a defined return period, such as 100 or 250 years.

Proportional Treaty Reinsurance   Agreement in which the insurer agrees to cede and the reinsurer agrees to accept a proportional share of all reinsurances offered within the limits of a treaty, as specified on the slip. Limits can be monetary, geographical, by branch, by class of business, or by some other measure. Reinsurers are obliged to accept all good and bad risks that fall within the scope of the treaty.

Quota Share Treaty Reinsurance   Agreement in which the ceding company is bound to cede and the reinsurer is bound to accept a fixed proportion of every risk accepted by the ceding company. The reinsurer shares proportionally in all losses and receives the same proportion of all premiums as the insurer, less commission. A quota share often specifies a monetary limit over which the reinsurer will not be committed on any one risk (for example, 70 percent of each risk, not to exceed $700,000 any one risk).

Rapid-onset Shock   Sudden shock, such as a flood, hurricane, frost, freeze, storm, or large change in a commodity price.

Rate on Line   Rate of premium for a reinsurance contract that, if applied to the reinsurer's liability, will result in an annual premium sufficient to meet expected losses over a number of years.

Regulatory Risk   Risk generated by unexpected changes in regulations, especially in import and export regimes, that affect producers' activities and profits.

Reinsurance   Insurance of insurance, used to smooth an insurance company's income over time, limit its exposure to individual risks and restrict losses, and increase its solvency margin (percent of capital and reserves to net premium income).

Risk Aggregation   Process of creating a risk-sharing arrangement that pools risks, thereby reducing transactions costs and giving small households or other participants a stronger bargaining position.

Risk Assessment   Qualitative and quantitative evaluation of risk. Process includes describing potential adverse effects, evaluating the magnitude of each risk, estimating potential exposure to the risk, estimating the range of likely effects given the likely exposures, and assessing uncertainties.

Risk Coping   Strategies employed to cope with a shock after it occurs. Examples of risk-coping strategies include selling assets, seeking additional employment, and applying for social assistance.

Risk Financing   Process of managing risk and the consequences of residual risk through products such as insurance contracts, catastrophe bonds, reinsurance, and options.

Risk Layering   Process of separating risk into tiers in order to finance and manage risk efficiently. Individuals can retain small but recurrent losses, which can be managed through risk mitigation techniques and self-insurance. More severe but less frequent losses can be transferred to cooperative/mutual insurance schemes, commercial insurers, and reinsurers. Governments often assume responsibility after major disasters, acting as reinsurers of last resort and providing postdisaster aid

Risk Management   Actions—including physical mechanisms (spraying a crop against aphids, using hail netting, planting windbreaks) and financial mechanisms (hedging, insurance, self-insurance)—taken to prevent or reduce losses caused by undesirable events.

Risk Mitigation   Actions taken to reduce the probability or impact of a risk event or exposure to risk events.

Risk Pooling   Aggregation of individual risks for the purpose of managing the consequences of independent risks. Pooling large numbers of homogenous, independent exposure units can produce an average loss that is close to the expected loss. It provides a statistically accurate prediction of future losses and helps determine premium rates.

Risk Retention   Process in which a party holds on to the financial responsibility for loss in the event of a shock.

Risk Transfer   Process of shifting the burden of financial loss or responsibility for risk financing to another party, through insurance, reinsurance, legislation, or other means.

Shock   Unexpected traumatic event, such as loss of land or livestock, caused by catastrophic weather events or other unexpected phenomena. A price shock occurs when the price of a commodity changes dramatically.

Slip   Document, usually prepared by a broker and submitted to underwriters, outlining the terms and conditions of an insurance proposal.

Slow-onset Shock   Shock, such as drought, that unfolds slowly and whose impact is difficult to assess or may not be recognized until high losses are incurred.

Social Safety Net   Various services, usually provided by the government, designed to prevent individuals or households from falling below a certain level of poverty. Such services include free or subsidized health care, child care, housing, and food as well as cash payments to people in need.

Stop-loss Treaty Reinsurance   Policy that covers claims once they exceed a certain amount. A policy with a stop-loss provision is a nonproportional type of reinsurance, in which the reinsurer agrees to pay the reinsured for losses that exceed a specified limit arising from any risk or any one event. For example, a reinsurer may agree to pay claims of $200,000 in excess of $100,000. If the claims are more than $300,000, the reinsured (that is, the insurer) will have to bear the remainder of the claims or make additional financing arrangements to cover the remaining risk exposure.

Transactions Costs   Costs, including the cost and time spent obtaining information, required to engage in an economic exchange. Transactions costs in insurance include those associated with underwriting, contract design, rate-making, adverse selection, and moral hazard.

Underwrite   To select or rate risks for insurance purposes.

Weather Index Insurance   Contingent claims contracts for which payouts are determined by an objective weather parameter (such as rainfall, temperature, or soil moisture) that is highly correlated with farm-level yields or revenue outcomes. See also *Index insurance*.

Yield Risk   Risk associated with the inability of an agricultural producer to predict the volume of output a production process will yield, because of external factors such as weather, pests, and diseases.

Overview

Governments in developing countries have been increasingly involved in the support of commercial agricultural (crop and livestock) insurance programs in recent years. A striking example is China, where, with support (and premium subsidies) from the central and provincial governments, the agricultural insurance market grew dramatically to become the second largest market in the world (after the United States) in 2008. In India and Mexico, weather-based crop insurance has been developed on a large scale to protect farmers against the vagaries of the weather. Many other countries have investigated the feasibility of agricultural insurance, and some have implemented pilot programs.

One common feature of many agricultural insurance programs is public support for agricultural insurance. With some rare exceptions, such as the hail insurance market, governments are supporting the development and particularly the expansion of agricultural insurance, often by subsidizing premiums.

In their attempt to design and implement agricultural insurance, many governments in developing countries have sought technical assistance from the international community, including the World Bank. The Bank is one of the few international financial organizations that has a fully dedicated insurance team of agricultural insurance experts, who currently provide technical assistance in more than 20 countries.

A recurrent request from governments is for information on the international experience with agricultural insurance, not only in developed countries, in some of which agricultural insurance has been offered for more than a century, but also in middle- and low-income countries. In particular, there is interest in the experience of public support for agricultural insurance, including its technical, operational, financial, and institutional aspects.

This book aims to inform and update public and private decision makers involved in promoting agricultural insurance about recent developments in agriculture insurance. The literature is heavily biased toward the practice and experience of a few very large public-private programs in Northern America and Europe, which are driven by large public financial subsidies. This book provides decision makers with a framework for developing agricultural insurance. It is based on an analytical review of the rationale for public intervention in agricultural insurance and a detailed comparative analysis of crop and livestock insurance programs provided with and without government support in more than 65 developed and developing countries. The comparative analysis is based on a survey conducted by the World Bank's agricultural insurance team in 2008. Drawing on the survey results, the book identifies some key roles governments can play to support the development of sustainable, affordable, and cost-effective agricultural insurance programs.

The book does not provide decision makers with a prescriptive model for government-supported agricultural insurance, nor does it prescribe the specific support and intervention roles that government should adopt in order to promote the development of commercially sustainable agricultural insurance in their countries. The book does not provide a detailed technical analysis of the different types of traditional indemnity-based and new weather index crop insurance products and programs adopted in the 65 countries covered by the World Bank survey. Rather, the book is designed to provide policymakers with an updated picture of the spectrum of institutional frameworks and experiences with agricultural insurance, ranging from countries in which the public sector provides no support to those in which governments heavily subsidize agricultural insurance. The book provides some simple financial performance indicators and comparisons between country programs that subsidize and those that do not subsidize premiums. It is hoped that the book will stimulate debate among local government, local insurance companies, international reinsurers, and aid agencies on the role of government support in promoting the introduction and development of market-based and commercially sustainable agricultural insurance in developing countries.

Why Should Governments Support Agricultural Insurance?

Market and regulatory impediments are often invoked to justify public intervention in the provision of agricultural insurance. Governments should identify and address these impediments, described briefly below, to help farmers complement their risk management activities with potentially cost-effective financial tools such as insurance.

Systemic Risk

One of the central arguments for government intervention in the provision, administration, and oversight of agricultural insurance programs involves the presence of systemic risk (that is, risk that affects a large number of economic units, such as farmers and herders, simultaneously). The systemic component of agricultural risks can generate major losses in the portfolio of agricultural insurers. Estimated probable maximum losses for major events, such as those occurring once every hundred years, may exceed average expected losses by many times and seriously affect the financial solvency of insurance companies. Public intervention would be justified because no private reinsurer or pool of reinsurers has the capacity to cover such a large liability when the risks, even though small, may be difficult to diversify.

Informational Asymmetries

The two critical informational problems that any insurance program faces are adverse selection and moral hazard. They are intimately tied to the difficulties associated with measuring risks and monitoring farmer behavior. It may be very difficult for private entities to measure risks, collect relevant data, monitor producer behavior, and establish and enforce underwriting guidelines. These difficulties can result in high, sometimes prohibitive, transactions costs that preclude the development of private insurance markets. Governments have a major role to play in reducing informational asymmetry. The development and maintenance of agricultural and weather databases as public goods can help insurers properly design and price agricultural insurance contracts, thus reducing adverse selection. Public extension services assisting and supervising farmers in the management of their production risks before and after the occurrence of a loss can help reduce moral hazard.

Postdisaster Assistance Programs

Governments tend to alleviate the effects of crop failures or other disasters by providing postdisaster direct compensation as a relief measure. This poses a "Samaritan's dilemma," whereby postdisaster aid discourages programs such as insurance, which provide more-efficient financial solutions and reduce the magnitude of losses from future events.

Limited Access to International Reinsurance Markets

Access to the international reinsurance market is often limited in developing countries, particularly for specialized lines of business such as agricultural insurance. In recent years, agricultural reinsurers and brokers have shown increasing interest in developing their business in low- and middle-income countries, particularly in large countries such as China and India. Smaller countries with far fewer business opportunities may have more difficulty attracting these international companies. Reinsurers report that reinsurance capacity is available for crop and livestock programs that are properly designed and have rates that generate sufficient premium volume to cover expected losses, operating costs, and cost of capital (including profit).

Agricultural Risk Market Infrastructure

An important supply-side impediment to the provision of agricultural insurance in developing countries is the lack of infrastructure support for agricultural insurance. Government could create these public goods, such as agricultural and weather databases and crop risk models, providing domestic agricultural insurers with reliable data and quantitative tools to better assess their catastrophe risk exposure and thus design actuarially sound agricultural insurance products.

Low Risk Awareness

Farmers tend to be very aware of their production risks. They may exhibit "cognitive failure," however, in that they may underestimate the likelihood or severity of catastrophic events. Stakeholder consultations in India and Mongolia reveal that farmers and herders recall the occurrence of major past events but tend to underestimate their severity. Governments may play an important role in providing farmer awareness and education programs and in supporting the marketing and promotion programs of the private commercial insurance sector.

Lack of Insurance Culture

A commonly cited reason for the low demand for agricultural insurance in developing countries is the limited understanding of its benefits. Insurance is often perceived as a nonviable investment, because premiums are collected every year but indemnities are paid much less frequently. The general population views insurance—particularly agricultural insurance, which, by definition, pays only when infrequent events occur coverage—as a privilege of the rich.

Regulatory Impediments

The regulatory frameworks governing insurance markets in many low- and middle-income countries tend to be underdeveloped. As a result, regulatory overlay can in some cases inhibit increased penetration of insurance, including agricultural insurance. Innovative agricultural insurance products, such as index-based crop insurance or parametric (weather-based) crop insurance, require an enabling regulatory framework.

What Can We Learn from International Experience?

More than half of all countries—104 countries—offered some form of agricultural insurance in 2008. In 2008 the World Bank conducted a survey on agricultural insurance programs in 65 countries, covering 52 percent of high-income countries, 69 percent of middle-income countries, and 50 percent of low-income countries that are known to offer some form of agricultural insurance (figure 1). The key objectives of the survey were to update international experience with public and private agricultural insurance in developed and developing economies and to examine the different ways in which governments support or do not support agricultural insurance. The survey provides a good overview of agricultural insurance markets worldwide, particularly in low- and middle-income countries, the primary focus of this book.

Most developing countries witnessed a shift from public to market-based agricultural insurance since the 1990s. The period 1950–90 saw a major growth in public sector multiple peril crop insurance programs (MPCI), particularly in Latin America and in Asia. Historically, these programs have performed very poorly. Since the 1990s, governments have promoted agricultural insurance through the commercial insurance sector, often under public-private partnerships (PPPs). As of 2008, private insurance providers operated in 54 percent of the surveyed countries, and PPPs were implemented in 37 percent of them. The development of the private agricultural insurance sector increases with the development level. Coinsurance pools, usually relying on PPPs, have been established, mainly in middle-income countries, as a way to strengthen the supply of agricultural insurance.

Global agricultural premium volume increased dramatically between 2004 and 2007, rising from $8 billion to about $20 billion, $15 billion of which is captured by the World Bank survey (table 1). This stunning increase was caused by rising agricultural commodity prices and sum insured values on which premium was paid; the expansion of agricultural insurance in China, Brazil, and Eastern Europe; and increasing government subsidy support in major countries, including Brazil, China, the Republic of Korea, Turkey, and the United States.

Despite this recent growth, penetration is still much lower than non–life insurance penetration in most countries. Agricultural insurance

Figure 1 Availability of Agricultural Insurance in 2008

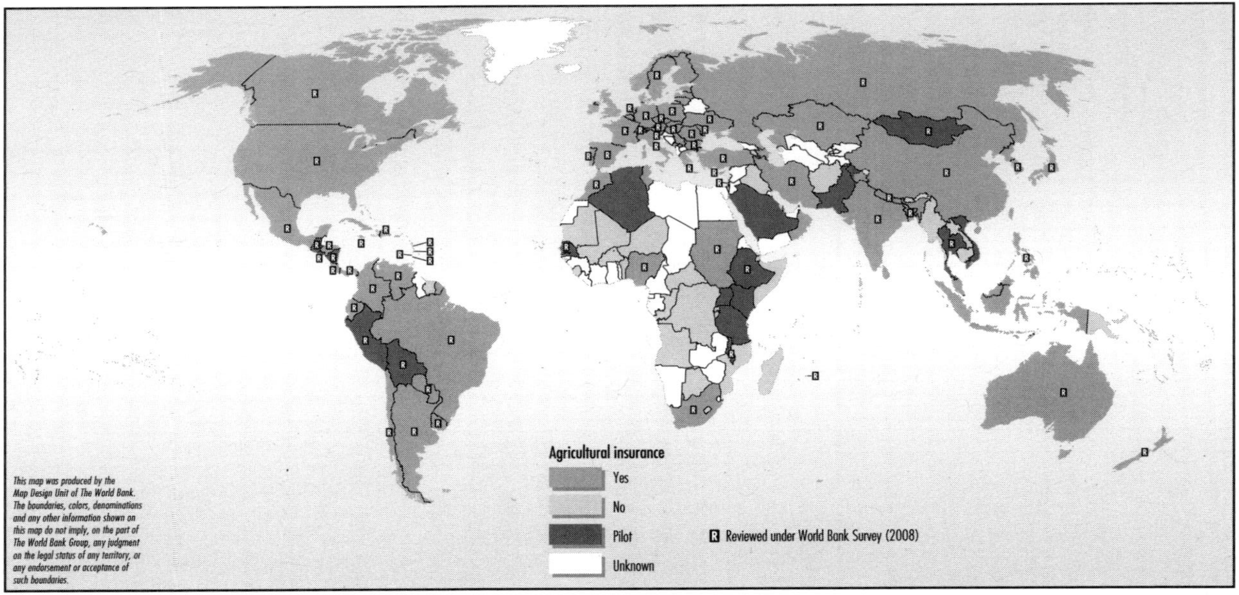

Agricultural insurance

- Yes
- No
- Pilot
- Unknown

R Reviewed under World Bank Survey (2008)

This map was produced by the
Map Design Unit of The World Bank.
The boundaries, colors, denominations
and any other information shown on
this map do not imply, on the part of
The World Bank Group, any judgment
on the legal status of any territory, or
any endorsement or acceptance of
such boundaries.

Source: World Bank Survey 2008.

Table 1 Estimated 2007 Agricultural Insurance Premiums, by Country Development Status

Development status	Number of countries	Estimated crop premiums ($ million)	Estimated livestock premiums ($ million)	Estimated agricultural premiums ($ million)	Percentage of global agricultural premiums	Agriculture insurance penetration (premiums as a percentage of 2007 agricultural GDP)
High-Income	21	11,869.0	1,192.3	13,061.3	86.5	2.3
Upper Middle-Income	18	872.6	40.1	912.7	6.0	0.3
Lower Middle-Income	20	789.3	334.1	1,123.5	7.4	0.2
Low-Income	6	0.2	4.8	5.0	0.0	0.0
All Countries	65	13,531.1	1,571.4	15,102.4	100.0	0.9

Source: World Bank Survey 2008.

penetration rate is expressed as the ratio between agricultural insurance premium volume and agricultural GDP; non–life insurance penetration is expressed as the ratio between non–life insurance premium volume and GDP. The agricultural insurance penetration rate is lower than the non–life insurance penetration in all groups of countries classified by development status. The gap decreases with development level.

Agricultural insurance takes a long time to take off. The United States and many European countries have had some form of crop or livestock insurance for more than a century and are mature markets with high penetration rates. In contrast, in many developing countries, agricultural insurance has been operating for only 5–10 years (even less in countries introducing index-based insurance), and agricultural insurance demand and uptake have yet to take off.

Agricultural insurance provision is dominated by high-income countries and China. Almost 90 percent of global agricultural insurance premium volume is underwritten in high-income countries. In 2008 the agricultural insurance premium volume in China was estimated at $1.75 billion, making this middle-income country the second-largest agricultural insurance market after the United States.

Agricultural insurance provision is largely dominated by crop insurance. The World Bank survey captures about 80 percent of the estimated global agricultural insurance premium volume (an even higher percentage in low- and middle-income countries). This survey is therefore representative of the global market. It shows that 91 percent of the agricultural insurance business by premium volume comes from crop insurance.

Traditional named-peril crop insurance and MPCI are the two main lines of the agricultural insurance business. Named-peril crop insurance (such as hail insurance) is underwritten in all of the high-income surveyed countries but in less than half of the surveyed developing countries (figure 2). Major advantages of named-peril crop insurance include the low-cost damage-based indemnity system, the restriction to key perils, and the affordability of premiums.

Individual-grower MPCI is available in about half of the high-income and almost 80 percent of the middle-income countries, particularly in Latin America. This yield-based indemnity product is much more complex, usually with higher premium rates, because it generally provides all-risk cover for the insured crop and is more costly to administer, because it requires preinspections and in-field measurement of crop yields in order to assess losses. International experience throughout the world shows that individual-farmer MPCI can be subject to adverse selection and moral hazard.

Figure 2 Availability of Crop Insurance Products in 2008 among Countries with Agricultural Insurance, by Development Status

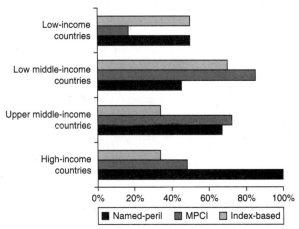

Source: World Bank Survey 2008.

Index-based crop insurance is available, mainly at a pilot stage, in one out of three surveyed countries. Such insurance—in which indemnity payments are based on an index (such as cumulative rainfall or aggregate crop yields in a geographical area)—is available in 20 percent of high-income and more than 40 percent of middle-income countries, usually under weather-based crop insurance programs. The aggregate premium volume for index insurance remains very low, however, as markets are not mature. Except in India and Mexico, most of the weather-based crop insurance programs are still under pilot implementation, with only few farmers insured. Many index initiatives in middle- and low-income countries have been supported by the donor community and the international reinsurance market.

Livestock insurance is available in 85 percent of the surveyed countries. It is offered, usually in the form of individual animal accident and mortality cover, in a very high proportion of the surveyed countries. Many programs are very small, however, with demand and penetration rates generally low. Consequently, premium volume is much lower for livestock insurance than for crop insurance. Almost 80 percent of high-income and 63 percent of low- and middle-income countries surveyed offer livestock insurance. Insurance against epidemic diseases is offered mainly in high-income countries. Countries with large and specialized livestock insurance markets include China, Germany, Mexico, and Spain. Mongolia has been piloting index-based livestock insurance since 2006.

Delivery channels are highly dependent on the development status of private insurance markets. In developed insurance markets in high-income and upper-middle-income countries, insurance is traditionally marketed through insurance agents employed by insurance companies or insurance brokers. In low-income countries, where the insurance market is underdeveloped, agricultural insurance is provided mainly through cooperatives and farmers' groups. The provision of agricultural insurance through rural banking networks, including microfinance institutions, is still very limited, although several initiatives are under preparation in Africa and Asia.

Almost 80 percent of agricultural insurance programs are offered on a voluntary basis. In lower-middle- and low-income countries, agricultural insurance is often compulsory for borrowers of agricultural loans. This type of credit-linked insurance may offer new opportunities to develop agricultural insurance in middle- and low-income countries.

Agricultural reinsurance is purchased mainly from private reinsurers. It is usually critical for domestic agricultural insurers to secure enough risk capital in case of a major disaster causing catastrophic insurance losses. In two-thirds of the surveyed countries, the provision of agricultural reinsurance is from private reinsurers. In 22 percent of the surveyed countries, agricultural reinsurance is provided by both public and private entities. Some countries (including Costa Rica, Iran, Japan, and Kazakhstan) rely only on public reinsurance.

Premium subsidies are the most common form of public intervention in agricultural insurance. Almost two-thirds of the surveyed countries (at all levels of development) provide agricultural insurance premium subsidies, with subsidies usually on the order of 50 percent of the original gross premium. Some countries also offer variable premium subsidies. A few countries, such as India, cap premiums. Premium subsidy programs are offered mainly under MPCI or area-yield insurance (a major exception is South Africa, which offers nonsubsidized MPCI to individual farmers). Most named-peril crop insurance products, such as hail insurance, have been offered for many years without any public subsidies. Government intervention in livestock insurance is much lower than for crop insurance: only 35 percent of the surveyed countries offer livestock insurance premium subsidies.

Governments also provide public reinsurance (32 percent of surveyed countries), subsidies on administrative and operational expenses (16 percent), and loss adjustment subsidies (6 percent). Public sector support to reinsurance is higher in high-income than middle-income economies. Forms of support range from national reinsurance companies to agreements under which governments act as excess-of-loss reinsurers (in such cases, the government charges no reinsurance premium). Governments can also provide support with legislation (51 percent of crop programs and 33 percent of livestock programs reviewed) and research, development, and training (44 percent of crop programs and 33 percent of livestock programs reviewed).

Only 11 percent of the surveyed countries have developed special programs for small and marginal farmers, usually in the form of additional premium subsidies. In some countries, such as Chile, rural banks and insurance companies have developed such programs. In Mexico the public reinsurance company supports small farmers' self-insurance groups.

The total public cost of agricultural insurance programs is estimated at 68 percent of the 2007 global premium volume, of which upfront premium subsidies represent 44 percent. On the basis of the World Bank survey in 65 countries, the overall government cost of upfront premium subsidies is estimated at 44 percent of original gross premiums. With the inclusion of administrative and operating subsidies and claim subsidies, the total cost to governments of agricultural insurance provision may be as high as 68 percent of original gross premiums.

The public cost of agricultural insurance subsidies represents 50–300 percent of the premiums paid by farmers in the majority of the countries surveyed. Public support to agricultural insurance in many high-income countries (including Italy, Spain, and the United States) represents more than twice the premium paid by farmers. In contrast, in most of the middle- and low-income countries surveyed, public support to agricultural insurance represents 50–150 percent of the premium paid by farmers (figure 3).

Subsidies are not always a precondition for high penetration. High levels of agricultural insurance uptake can be found not only for programs that carry high premium subsidy levels (such as MPCI in Canada, India, and the United States) but also in countries that have strong traditions in agricultural insurance through unsubsidized named-peril crop insurance and livestock insurance (such as Argentina, Australia, and Germany). The survey results thus do not support the argument that premium subsidies are a precondition for farmers and herders to purchase agricultural insurance.

PPPs in agricultural insurance tend to improve the financial performance of government-sponsored agricultural insurance programs. Loss ratios (a simple measure of the financial performance of an insurance program) seem to be lower when programs are managed by the private sector, sometimes with support from the government through PPPs. This may be a consequence of better implementation of insurance principles, such as sound underwriting procedures and better pricing of risk; lower administrative costs; and greater financial discipline of private insurers.

Figure 3 Government Subsidies as Percentage of 2007 Premium Paid by Producers in Selected Countries

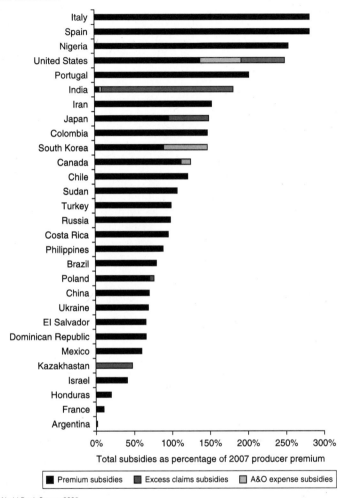

Total subsidies as percentage of 2007 producer premium

■ Premium subsidies   ▦ Excess claims subsidies   ▢ A&O expense subsidies

Source: World Bank Survey 2008.
Note: The producer premium is the share of total premium paid by the farmer after deduction of premium subsidies. Excess claims subsidies in Kazakhstan are based on a three-year average for 2004–07. The figure for the United States excludes private crop hail insurance.

How Should Governments Support Agricultural Insurance?

Where it is offered, public support to agricultural insurance is part of the government's overall agricultural policy, which may seek to correct market and regulatory inefficiencies and be part of broader objectives.

Each agricultural insurance program is unique and requires tailor-made solutions. That said, several key features emerge that governments may want to consider when designing and implementing agricultural insurance.

Agricultural insurance is part of a comprehensive agricultural risk management framework. It can contribute to the modernization of agriculture. However, it cannot operate in isolation. It should be promoted only when basic agricultural services—such as timely availability of inputs, extension services, and efficient marketing channels for agricultural outputs—are in place.

Agricultural insurance programs need to be customized to beneficiaries. The emerging commercial agricultural sector needs more standardized insurance products offered through cooperatives or rural finance institutions, such as credit-linked agricultural insurance. The traditional farming sector may not be geared toward commercial insurance; governments may therefore need to consider alternative support mechanisms, in the form of social safety net schemes, for example.

Agricultural insurance is a complex line of business that requires highly technical expertise, both in development and operational phases. Private insurance markets have proved to be efficient, without public intervention, for dealing with nonsystemic risk and large farmers, but purely commercial insurance may not be viable for systemic risks or smaller farmers. The primary role of governments should be to address market and regulatory imperfections in order to encourage participation by the private insurance and reinsurance industry.

In competitive markets, insurance premiums should be risk based and differentiated, thus reflecting the underlying risk exposure. Actuarially sound rates draw attention to the agricultural production risk exposure of individuals, firms, or governments and allow them to evaluate the benefits of agricultural risk management programs by comparing the cost of risk reduction investments with the resulting reduction in potential losses. They inform farmers and herders about their risk exposure and provide them with incentives to invest in risk mitigation activities (for example, irrigation) or to shift from nonviable crops to more viable crops. Risk-based premiums can also assist governments in the financial planning of agricultural losses through improved assessment of their contingent liability. By understanding their exposure, governments can better assess their liabilities in case of natural calamities and devise appropriate financial strategies.

Governments must carefully analyze the fiscal implications of government-sponsored agricultural insurance programs, whose costs may not be sustainable in the long term. Subsidies on agricultural insurance premiums should be carefully considered, because they can distort price signals and provide inappropriate incentives to farmers and herders to invest in unprofitable farming activities. The World Bank survey does not support the argument that premium subsidies are always a prerequisite if farmers and livestock breeders are to purchase voluntary crop and livestock insurance, as shown by several named-peril crop insurance programs. Where subsidies are offered, planners should carefully identify which beneficiaries, crop or livestock sectors, and regions to target and whether the subsidies will be provided for a limited period or phased out over time once agricultural insurance takes off and achieves a critical presence in the market.

In start-up situations, where market infrastructure is not yet developed, a technical support unit could be established to provide specialized services to agricultural insurance companies and other risk-pooling vehicles. This unit should have support from the government, insurers, and reinsurers. It could be either a stand-alone entity or hosted by an insurance provider (such as agricultural insurance pools or monopoly insurer). The goals of the technical support unit would include the following:

- Create a center of expertise able to support the development and scaling up of agricultural insurance.

- Establish a core team of agricultural insurance experts to provide technical support to agricultural insurers in underwriting, product development, pricing, product delivery, loss adjustment, catastrophe risk financing, and so forth.

- Create and manage a centralized database of agricultural and weather statistics, and make the database available to agricultural insurance practitioners.

- Promote the exchange of expertise among insurance companies and access to international best practice through training courses, operations manuals, and other means.

CHAPTER 1

Introduction

A griculture is a major economic sector and a critical source of livelihood in many developing countries. It is particularly exposed to adverse natural events, such as droughts or floods, and the economic costs of major disasters may even increase further in the future because of climate change. Farmers and herders have developed risk management strategies to cope with these adverse events, sometimes with the assistance of the governments. Agricultural insurance is one of the financial tools that agricultural producers can potentially use.

This chapter discusses how agricultural insurance can complement and enhance agricultural risk management activities and reviews the availability of agricultural insurance worldwide. Finally, it presents the objectives of this study, based in part on a survey of agricultural insurance programs in 65 countries.

Agricultural insurance is one of the financial tools agricultural producers can use to mitigate the risks associated with adverse natural events—events that climate change may render more frequent and more severe in the future. This chapter describes the importance of agriculture in developing countries, explains how agricultural insurance can complement and enhance other agricultural risk management activities, reviews the availability of agricultural insurance worldwide, and identifies the objectives of this study and the organization of this volume.

Agriculture in Developing Countries

Agriculture remains an important economic sector in many developing countries. It is a source of growth and a potential source of investment opportunities for the private sector. Two-thirds of the world's agricultural value added is estimated to be created in developing countries (World Bank 2008). In agriculture-based economies, which include most of Sub-Saharan Africa, agriculture generates 29 percent of GDP on average. In transforming countries—countries in which agriculture is no longer a major source of economic growth, which include most of South and East Asia and the Middle East and North Africa—the contribution of agriculture to GDP is much lower (table 1.1).

Nearly half of the world's population—some 2.9 billion people—live in rural areas. Agriculture is a source of livelihood for an estimated 86 percent of these people (World Bank 2008). Agriculture provides employment to 68 percent of the population in agriculture-based countries and 48 percent in transforming economies. About 94 percent of rural households live from their agricultural activities in agricultural-based countries; this proportion falls to 76 percent in transforming economies.

Many developing countries have seen major shifts in their agricultural policies toward the modernization of the agricultural sector over the past two decades. The change in policy contributed to more sustainable growth of the sector, although growth was slower than in nonagricultural sectors, except in agriculture-based countries (figure 1.1).

Agriculture can contribute to spurring growth, reducing poverty, and sustaining the environment. GDP growth in agriculture is at least twice as effective in reducing poverty as nonagricultural GDP growth (World Bank

Table 1.1 Share of Agriculture in Developing Countries (percent, except where otherwise indicated)

Item	Agriculture-based countries	Transforming countries	Urbanized countries
Rural population (millions)	417	2,220	255
Share of rural population	68	63	26
Share of agriculture in employment	64	48	16
Share of agriculture in GDP	29	13	6

Source: World Bank 2008; FAOStat.

Figure 1.1 Annual GDP Growth in Developing Countries, 1993–2005

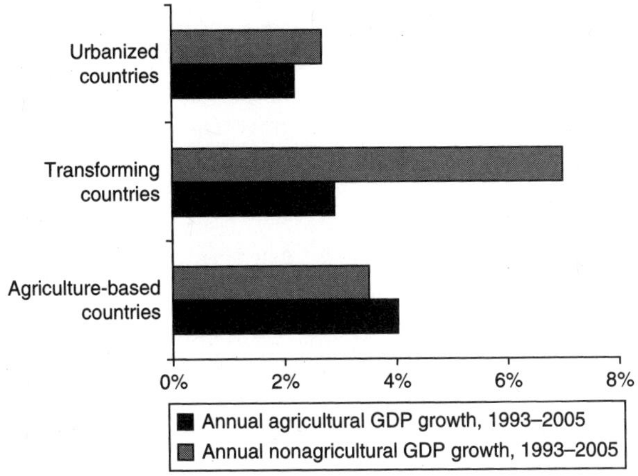

Source: World Bank 2008.

2008). The growth strategy for most agriculture-based economies should therefore be anchored in improving the productivity of the agricultural sector, particularly of food staples. Agricultural risk management, including agricultural insurance, can contribute to raising the productivity of agriculture by helping farmers and herders invest in more productive, but sometimes riskier, agricultural business activities.

Risk Management in Agriculture

Agricultural producers face a myriad of risks that can threaten their output, their income, and ultimately their consumption. Although any taxonomy can be arbitrary, the main sources of risk can be classified as shown in table 1.2. Farmers and herders face a range of risks, including idiosyncratic risks (such as fire, hail, and health), which affect them independently, and systemic risks (such as drought, epidemic diseases, and price), which affect a large number of producers at the same time.

The extent to which agricultural producers are averse to risk plays a key role in their risk management decisions, including their demand for agricultural insurance. Although most economic models and theories assume that agents are averse to risk, empirical analyses show a wide dispersion of

Table 1.2 Classification of Risks Facing Agricultural Producers

Type of risk	Idiosyncratic ◄——————————————► Systemic		
Natural disaster	Hail	Flood, pest infestation	Drought
Diseases and pests			Contagious animal disease
Price			Commodity, inputs, exchange rates
Financial			Interest rates
Operational		Availability of inputs	Evolution of production techniques (for example, biotechnology)
Environmental		Pollution, deforestation	
Policy			Public subsidies, agricultural policy
Health	Illness, injury, disability	Epidemic diseases	
Property	Fire, theft		Earthquake, floods

Source: Authors, adapted from Holzmann and Jorgensen 2000.

risk preferences. Moscardi and de Janvry (1977) find considerable risk aversion in a sample of small Mexican subsistence farmers. Binswanger (1980) shows that wealthier, better-educated, and more progressive farmers tend to be less risk averse. Goodwin's (2001) study based on a survey of 593 U.S. farmers finds that they can be risk neutral or even risk preferring.

A vast body of literature examines how agricultural producers in developing countries manage their risk exposure (see, for example, Holzmann and Jorgensen 2000; Anderson 2001; Varangis, Larson, and Anderson 2002; Gurenko and Mahul 2004; World Bank 2005). Farmers can use various tools, where they are available, to deal with these multiple sources of risk.

It is common to differentiate risk reduction strategies into two main categories: risk management and risk coping. Risk management strategies attempt to address risk ex ante; risk coping strategies address risk ex post. One can also differentiate between technical and financial risk management approaches (table 1.3). Agricultural insurance is typically one of many tools that farmers and herders can use as part of their comprehensive agricultural risk management strategy.

Developing countries vary significantly in the extent to which they protect their agricultural sectors against agricultural risks. Countries

Table 1.3 Examples of Technical and Financial Risk Management Mechanisms

Type of risk management	Examples
Technical	Low-risk production
	Irrigation
	Pest prevention (pesticides, herbicides)
	Livestock disease prevention (vaccination)
	On-farm diversification (crop rotation)
	Off-farm diversification
Financial	Insurance
	Hedging
	Precautionary savings
	Contingent borrowing

Source: Authors, based on Anderson 2001.

in which financial markets are underdeveloped rely heavily on self-insurance and postdisaster aid. As financial markets become more sophisticated, price hedging and agricultural insurance often complement postdisaster assistance.

To help countries develop sustainable and cost-effective agricultural insurance programs, the World Bank supports a country agricultural insurance framework that is based partly on corporate risk management but that also considers economic and social factors, such as the government's fiscal profile and the living conditions of the poor. This framework is based on four pillars: agricultural risk assessment, agribusiness segmentation, agricultural risk financing, and institutional capacity building (see appendix B).

The management of agricultural production risks relies on the optimal combination of technical and financial tools. Farmers and herders can retain small but recurrent losses through appropriate on-farm risk mitigation techniques (such as irrigation and pest prevention) and self-insurance tools (such as savings and contingent credit). More severe but less frequent losses can be gradually transferred to cooperative/mutual insurance schemes, commercial insurers, and reinsurers. Governments, with the assistance of the international donor community, may have a major role to play in case of major disasters, acting as reinsurers of last resort and providing postdisaster aid (figure 1.2).

Figure 1.2 Agricultural Risk Layering

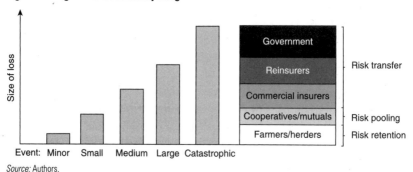

Source: Authors.

Agricultural Insurance

Between the 1950s and the 1980s, there was major growth in public sector multiple peril crop insurance (MPCI) programs in Latin America (for example, Brazil, Costa Rica, and Mexico) and Asia (for example, India, the Philippines), often linked to seasonal production credit programs for small farmers. Similar public programs were implemented in Europe (for example, Portugal and Spain) and the former Soviet Union. Since the 1990s, the poor performance of most public sector schemes and their limited uptake among farmers have led many governments to promote agricultural insurance through the private commercial sector, often backed by government financial support under public-private partnerships.

Agricultural insurance complements other instruments aimed at stabilizing producer incomes. Governments have traditionally put heavy emphasis on managing agricultural outputs and input markets as a means of stabilizing producer incomes, through marketing boards, quotas, price support mechanism, input subsidies, and other mechanisms. Governments perceive agricultural insurance as supplementing these traditional means by addressing production risks. With very few exceptions (such as agricultural revenue insurance products available in the United States), agricultural insurance does not cover price volatility.

Overall, government-sponsored MPCI programs have been disappointing. Limited insurance penetration despite high premium subsidies;

consistent underestimation of the catastrophic risks involved in agriculture; poor financial performance, with claims and administrative costs exceeding premiums; inappropriate pricing; uncontrolled moral hazard; and adverse selection are among the key endemic problems underlying agricultural insurance programs worldwide, in both developed and developing countries.

Hazell, Pomareda, and Valdes (1986) and Hazell (1992) review the experience of several crop insurance programs. They concluded that MPCI has fulfilled few of its objectives, mainly because administration costs are generally too high in relation to the benefits in risk reduction farmers receive. Wright and Hewitt (1994) suggest that the perceived demand for agricultural insurance may be overstated, because farmers can use diversification and savings to cushion the impact of production shortfalls on consumption.

Innovative insurance products, such as index-based insurance, offer new opportunities for agricultural insurance in developing countries, although their long-term sustainability has yet to be proved. Under index-based insurance, the indemnity payout is based on a verifiable and transparent index (such as the level of rainfall, the aggregate crop yield in a given area, or aggregate livestock mortality). The donor community and international development agencies have helped low- and middle-income countries develop such products to complement traditional indemnity-based products.

Agricultural (crop and livestock) insurance is currently available in more than 100 countries, either as well-developed programs or pilots (figure 1.3; see also appendix A). The majority of high-income countries (58 percent) have well-established agricultural insurance markets. In contrast, only 35 percent of low- and middle-income countries offer such products and programs. The availability of agricultural insurance is particularly low in low-income countries (8 percent). Pilot programs, which reach only a limited number of farmers and herders, are being implemented in various forms (including named-peril crop insurance, index-based crop insurance, or livestock insurance) in eight middle-income and eight low-income countries (table 1.4).

The incidence of agricultural insurance is highest in Latin American and the Caribbean. Only a few countries in Sub-Saharan Africa, including

Figure 1.3 Availability of Agricultural Insurance Worldwide, 2008

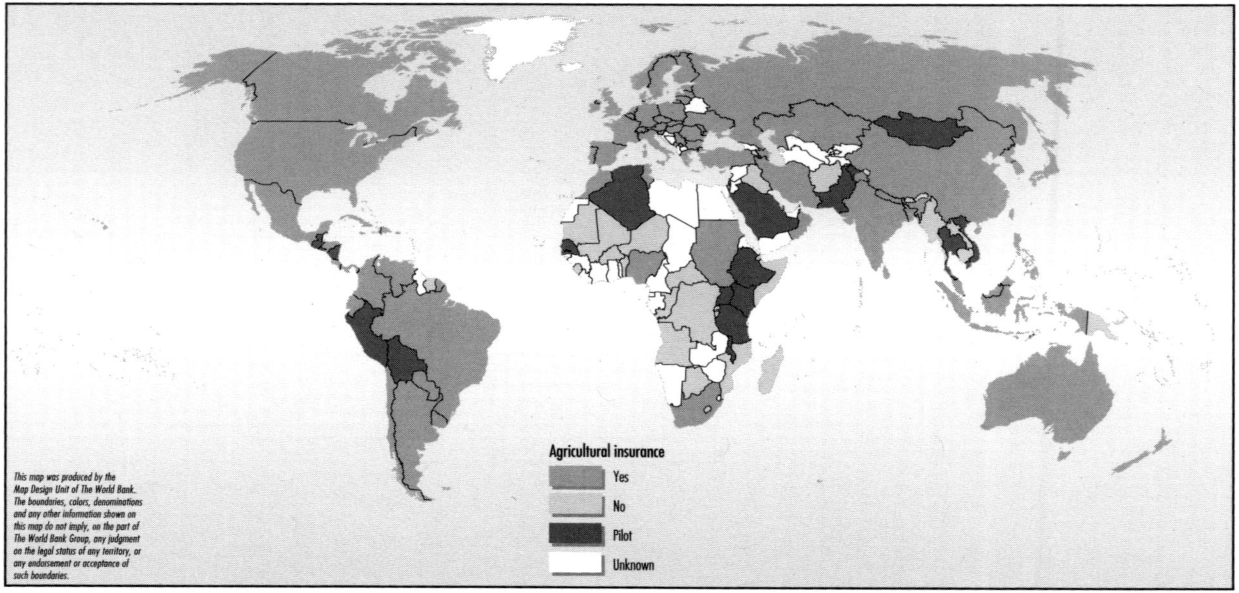

Agricultural insurance

- Yes
- No
- Pilot
- Unknown

This map was produced by the
Map Design Unit of The World Bank.
The boundaries, colors, denominations
and any other information shown on
this map do not imply, on the part of
The World Bank Group, any judgment
on the legal status of any territory, or
any endorsement or acceptance of
such boundaries.

Source: World Bank Survey 2008.

Table 1.4 Availability of Agricultural Insurance in 2008, by Development Status and Region

Item	Yes	No	Pilot	Unknown	Total
Development status					
High-income	38	8	2	17	65
Low- and middle-income	48	39	16	41	144
Low-income	4	21	8	16	49
Lower-middle-income	17	14	8	15	54
Upper-middle-income	27	4	0	10	41
Region					
East Asia and Pacific	5	10	3	5	23
Europe and Central Asia	13	1	0	10	24
Latin America and the Caribbean	19	3	5	2	29
Middle East and North Africa	3	2	1	7	13
South Asia	4	3	1	0	8
Sub-Saharan Africa	4	20	6	17	47
All countries	86	47	18	58	209

Source: World Bank Survey 2008.
Note: Agricultural insurance includes both crop and livestock insurance. See appendix A for the World Bank classification of countries by development status.

Mauritius, Nigeria, South Africa, and Sudan, are known to provide agricultural insurance.

Agricultural insurance has been offered in some industrial countries for more than a century. In contrast, the sector remains underserviced in low- and middle-income countries (figure 1.4). Penetration of agricultural insurance exceeds 1 percent in high-income countries but is still much lower than penetration of insurance products other than life insurance. In low- and middle- income countries, the agricultural insurance penetration is less than 0.3 percent. The gap between the penetration of non–life insurance and agricultural insurance increases as development status decreases.

Objectives of the Study

The World Bank has actively helped governments in low- and middle-income countries develop market-based agricultural crop and livestock insurance programs, including both traditional indemnity-based and new index-based insurance products. It is increasingly being asked to

Figure 1.4 Penetration of Agricultural and Non–Life Insurance, by Development Status 2007

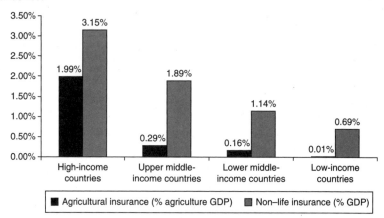

Source: Authors, based on Cummins and Mahul 2009; World Bank Survey 2008.
Note: Non–life insurance penetration is the ratio of the value of non–life insurance premiums to GDP, stated as a percentage. Agricultural insurance penetration is defined as the ratio of the value of agricultural premiums to agricultural GDP, stated as a percentage.

advise governments in developing countries on the best way to introduce agricultural insurance, the most appropriate institutional framework, and the specific roles that governments can or should play in promoting the widespread adoption of agricultural insurance. These programs rely mainly on PPPs and are included in broader efforts of agricultural risk management. They are often connected to agricultural finance support efforts and tied to complementary efforts in agricultural extension. The World Bank currently provides technical assistance for agricultural insurance in almost 20 countries. About half of the projects it supports (including projects in Central America, India, Malawi, Mongolia, and Thailand) are under pilot implementation.

Several governments in developing countries have recently tried to promote agricultural insurance, moving from small-scale pilots to large-scale agricultural insurance programs, mainly through the provision of agricultural premium subsidies. A striking example is China, where, with support (and premium subsidies) of central and provincial governments, the agricultural insurance market grew dramatically to become the second-largest market (after the United States) in 2008. Public support to agriculture aims at correcting market imperfections and can take many forms, including input subsidies, guaranteed output price, or subsidized interest rates on agricultural loans.

A variety of studies review the global agricultural insurance market supply (see, for example, Mapfre 1984, 1986; Hazell, Pomareda, and Valdes 1986; FAO 1991a, 1991b; UNCTAD 1994). They provide a detailed analysis of selected national agricultural insurance programs in terms of products offered, uptake, and financial performance.

Since these major contributions to the literature on agricultural insurance, the sector in developing countries has seen major changes, including market liberalization in agriculture, greater involvement of the private sector, innovations in insurance products and services, and climate change. More recent studies reexamine the agricultural insurance market, focusing mainly on European countries (see, for example, European Commission 2001, 2006) and selected middle-income countries (Swiss Re 2007).

This book provides an updated overview of the different institutional and organizational arrangements for agricultural insurance, the role of government support, and the types of government financial and other support, drawing especially on experience in low- and middle-income countries. It presents a comparative analysis based on a World Bank survey of agricultural insurance markets in 65 countries, with a focus on the role of government in developing or enhancing agricultural insurance. The survey, conducted in 2008, was designed to collect specific information on the institutional structure of agricultural insurance (including crop, livestock, and aquaculture) and, particularly, the role of governments; the type of agricultural insurers involved; and, in markets with public intervention, the type of public intervention and its public costs. The book provides recommendations for developing sustainable, affordable, and cost-effective agricultural insurance programs, examining the institutional, technical, operational, and financial challenges faced in doing so. The focus is on small and marginal farmers. Farmers face many other sources of risk, including price risk and health risk, which affect their income and ultimately their consumption. The scope of this book is limited to agricultural insurance, however, specifically, the role of government in the provision of agricultural insurance in low- and middle-income countries.

The volume is organized as follows. Chapter 2 discusses the economic rationale for public intervention in agricultural insurance, identifying various market and regulatory imperfections that may impede the development of sustainable programs. It also presents other reasons why governments may want to promote agricultural insurance, including the impact of climate change on agriculture, the modernization of the agricultural sector, and the need for better financial planning of adverse natural events.

Chapter 3 presents the results and key findings of the 2008 World Bank survey on provision of agricultural insurance. It describes the origins of and trends in agricultural insurance provision, reports on public intervention in agricultural insurance and agricultural insurance penetration around the world, and assesses the performance of agricultural insurance provided by both the public and private sectors.

Chapter 4 identifies challenges developing countries face supporting market-based agricultural insurance markets. It identifies options governments may want to consider for creating sustainable and competitive agricultural insurance and reinsurance markets.

The report includes five short technical appendixes. Appendix A overviews the availability of agricultural insurance worldwide. Appendix B describes the framework for financial risk management of agricultural production risks promoted by the World Bank. Appendix C reproduces the questionnaire used in the survey of agricultural insurance programs. Appendix D reports the results of the survey. Appendix E, available online, in the Publications and Research section of the Web site http://www.insuranceforthepoor.org, overviews 62 of the 65 countries included in the survey (for 3 countries insufficient information on which to prepare an overview was provided).

CHAPTER 2

The Economic Rationale for Public Intervention in Agricultural Insurance

P ublic intervention in agricultural insurance markets is no different from intervention in other markets. Such intervention may be intended to address real or perceived failures of the market. In such cases, the general economic welfare may be improved as a result of the intervention. Some degree of protection and special treatment of agriculture is common in both developed and developing countries.

A number of social and political objectives underlie many agricultural programs, usually stated in terms of the importance of agriculture to the general economy, the importance of "family farms," and the special place of food and fiber products in society. These appeals have led to deep, longstanding intervention and large transfers from taxpayers to agricultural producers, especially in developed countries. The rhetoric underlying such policies often invokes the "Jeffersonian ideal" view of agriculture, which argues that agriculture deserves favored political treatment because of its inherent goodness.

This chapter examines the rationale for public intervention in agricultural insurance. It identifies market and regulatory imperfections that can hamper the development (both the design and the implementation) of a sustainable agricultural insurance program. It then discusses how agricultural insurance can contribute to the modernization of agriculture by facilitating access to credit and the adoption of techno-logical innovations. Insurance can also help governments devise better financial planning against natural disasters. The chapter analyzes the cost of insurance, the role of premium subsidies, and the rationale for compulsory agricultural insurance.

The economic rationale for public intervention in agricultural insur-ance and the role of public management policies have been investigated in the literature. In their seminal book, Hazell, Pomareda, and Valdes (1986) provide the first comprehensive study of the role of public risk manage-ment policies, particularly of agricultural insurance, to deal with the problem of unstable farm incomes. In 1990 and 1991, the Food and Agri-culture Organization (FAO) published a comprehensive review of national agricultural insurance schemes, drawing some conclusions on the role of governments in promoting agricultural insurance. The most comprehen-sive study on agricultural insurance provision in developing countries is the 1994 survey by the United Nations Conference on Trade and Devel-opment (UNCTAD) of 44 developing countries, which provides useful insights into the status of crop, livestock, poultry, and aquaculture insur-ance provisions in these countries and associated issues of a technical, financial, and institutional nature. Wright and Hewitt (1994) provide a detailed economic analysis of all-risk multiple peril crop insurance (MPCI) yield shortfall programs. They claim that private agricultural insurance markets may fail because the costs of maintaining these markets imply unacceptably low average payouts relative to premiums—that is, the administrative and operating expenses of this line of business are unacceptably high. The European Commission (2006) conducted a detailed review of the agricultural insurance markets in Europe. A World Bank (2005) study discusses agricultural risk management, focusing on innovative index-based insurance solutions.

Market and Regulatory Imperfections

Market and regulatory impediments are often invoked to justify public intervention in the provision of agricultural insurance. Various demand- and supply-side market imperfections that have hindered the development of agricultural insurance are discussed below.

Systemic Risk

One of the most prominent arguments in favor of government intervention is that the provision, administration, and oversight of agricultural insurance programs involve systemic risk (such as widespread drought or floods that affect a large number of farmers simultaneously). This argument is advanced by, among others, Miranda and Glauber (1997). The argument relates, at least indirectly, to the degree and extent to which reinsurance can be obtained to cover the risks associated with widespread, though perhaps infrequent, losses. Many of the crop-yield risks faced by farmers come from the randomness induced by weather and natural growing conditions. Because such risks are typically realized over a large geographic area, catastrophic risks may be significant and difficult for insurers to diversify. Likewise, widespread animal epidemic diseases can simultaneously affect a large number of herders, generating major losses.

The systemic component of agricultural risks can generate major losses in the portfolio of agricultural insurers. Estimated probable maximum losses for major events, such as those occurring once every hundred years, exceed average expected losses by many times. For example, it is estimated that a widespread drought in India could generate insured crop-yield losses that are up to three times higher than the annual expected losses at the national level (World Bank 2007b). Analyses by the World Bank in China show that a hypothetical agricultural portfolio of various crops in three provinces (Xinjiang, Heilongjiang, and Hainan) would have a probable maximum loss of a once every hundred year event that is more than 2.5 times the average expected loss (World Bank 2007b). Probable maximum losses caused by livestock epidemics can be even higher, as shown by the outbreaks of foot-and-mouth disease in the United Kingdom in 2000 and more recently the avian flu epidemic. Although these peak risks are high, they are still reasonable compared with catastrophe risk exposure for earthquakes and hurricanes in property insurance, where extreme events can generate losses that exceed expected losses by factors of 50 or more (Cummins and Mahul 2009).

Public intervention is justified to insure against such losses because no private reinsurer or pool of reinsurers has the capacity to cover such a large liability when the risks, even though small, may be difficult to diversify. It is often noted that the one form of crop insurance for which private markets have flourished for more than a century without, or at least with very limited, public intervention, is insurance against hail, a risk that is largely nonsystemic and thus more diversifiable.

The notion that systemic risk is a source of market failure leads to the belief that, because private reinsurance markets may not be able to absorb the catastrophic risks associated with crops or livestock, the government should assume the role of a reinsurer of last resort. The government is assumed to have "deeper pockets" than private reinsurers and thus to be better able to provide the capital necessary to finance such systemic risks. The argument is persuasive, although many risks can be spread and diversified across different sectors by international reinsurers; the argument thus may be more accurately phrased in terms of the cost of reinsurance rather than whether any reinsurance can be obtained at any price. This line of business is marginal compared with other nonlife insurance lines. It is estimated that the value of worldwide agricultural insurance premiums represented only 1.1 percent of the value of worldwide nonlife insurance premiums in 2008.

Government intervention may boost the overall welfare of society by facilitating the purchase of some specific-peril insurance plans that address the risks associated with infectious or communicable hazards (Bekkerman, Goodwin, and Piggott 2008). In the case of plant or animal diseases that have the potential to spread and thereby cause more extensive damages than would be the case if immediate mitigation and measures were undertaken, the localized occurrence of a disease may threaten a much wider area. Because producers found to have the disease may be forced to destroy the commodity, suffering a significant, uncompensated loss, they face a strong incentive not to report infections or disease. If the government indemnifies farmers against the losses associated with infection, they have a much greater incentive to report the disease, thereby allowing protective and loss-mitigating actions to be taken. A clear role for the government exists in such cases. A public insurance or indemnification program may well serve the general welfare of society.

Informational Asymmetries

The two critical informational problems that any insurance program faces are adverse selection and moral hazard. Both are intimately tied to the difficulties associated with measuring risks and monitoring farmer behavior. It may be very difficult for private entities to measure risks, collect relevant data, monitor producer behavior, and establish and enforce underwriting guidelines. These difficulties result in high, possibly prohibitive, transactions costs that preclude the development of private insurance markets.

Adverse selection arises because of a lack of information, which in turn results in inaccurate premium rates that make high-risk individuals more likely to purchase insurance. Adverse selection can lead any insurance plan to be unprofitable and eventually fail. Avoiding adverse selection may require crop insurance programs to identify, acquire, and use data that discriminate among risks. Identifying homogeneous risk groups is a prerequisite for a successful contract. The governments may have a comparative advantage in providing additional information to help insurers discriminate their risks and price them accordingly. Policymakers may perceive such price differentiation as socially unacceptable, however.

Moral hazard occurs when insured agents alter their production practices in some way that changes their underlying risk and is not easily observable by insurers. In the case of agricultural insurance, this typically involves a failure to use good farming practices, to care for the crop, or to provide adequate fertilizer or water. Moral hazard is particularly acute under MPCI programs, where insurers may have difficulties distinguishing between losses caused by an adverse natural event and losses caused by bad management. This problem is particularly acute for crop pests and diseases. Traditional named-peril insurance, such as hail insurance, is much less exposed to moral hazard, because it is unpredictable and unavoidable (unless farmers use hail nets) and because the cause of loss can be more easily identified. The literature has extensively analyzed the impact of insurance on the use of agricultural inputs (see, for example, Horowitz and Lichtenberg 1993; Babcock and Hennessy 1996; Smith and Goodwin 1996). The results suggest that insurance reduces the use of agricultural chemicals.

The moral hazard problem has also been studied in developing countries. Breusted and Larson (2006) show that farmers' institutions such as the Fondos in Mexico can help manage moral hazard through peer monitoring, although they cannot eliminate it from an MPCI program. Hazell (1992), Skurai and Reardon (1997), and others identify strong potential demand for insurance in Sub-Saharan African countries, but their analysis raises concerns that moral hazard arising from postdisaster food aid may undermine the viability of such contracts.

Governments may have a major role to play in the reduction of informational asymmetry. The development and maintenance of agricultural and weather databases, as public goods, can help insurers properly design and price agricultural insurance contracts, thus reducing adverse selection. Public extension services that assist and supervise farmers in the management of their production risks before and after the occurrence of a loss can help reduce moral hazard.

Postdisaster Assistance Programs

Governments tend to alleviate the effects of crop failures or other disasters by providing postdisaster direct compensation as a relief measure. This poses a "Samaritan's dilemma" (Coate 1995), whereby postdisaster aid discourages programs that provide more efficient financial solutions and reduce the magnitude of losses from future events. Disaster payments are generally not an established set of programs (hence their ad hoc nature); they are usually emergency responses to specific loss events. A very wide range of disaster payment programs exist; in some cases, their frequency and magnitude suggest that they serve as a form of insurance.

Because disaster payments serve the same general purpose as insurance—providing compensation to indemnify losses—the existence of disaster payments may reduce farmer participation in crop insurance programs. Subtle issues relate to how these programs may bring about distortions that affect the performance of coincidental insurance programs. For example, disaster payments are usually triggered by widespread, large-scale losses that affect a majority of farmers in an area. If farmers are heterogeneous in terms of their risk and the risk underlying disasters is of a systemic nature, it is likely that those farmers who generally have low risk and only suffer losses when the events are widespread will be less willing to buy insurance. Provision of disaster payments may further skew participation in a crop insurance program toward higher-risk individuals, because low-risk farmers will count on protection from disaster payments. In this manner, disaster payments reinforce adverse selection problems. Many observers have noted that perennial disaster payments can have a major impact in reducing farmers' willingness to buy insurance (see Goodwin and Smith 1995 for a review of these issues within the context of the U.S. crop insurance and disaster relief programs).

The substitutability of disaster assistance programs and insurance programs has been discussed in the literature (see, for example, Wright and Hewitt 1994; Glauber 2007). Evidence against strong substitutability between crop insurance and disaster payments comes from the history of expenditures of the two programs. In the United States, for example, both programs have coexisted for more than 50 years, although the government initially justified crop insurance subsidies to promote crop insurance as a substitute for postdisaster assistance programs. In contrast, in Spain the law specifically excludes any postdisaster payments for natural disasters that are covered by the national agricultural insurance program.

Limited Access to the International Reinsurance Market

Access to the international reinsurance market is limited in developing countries, particularly for specialized lines of business, such as agricultural insurance. Many insurance companies in developing countries identify limited access as one of the main constraints to the development of agricultural insurance (see chapter 3). However, agricultural reinsurers and brokers have shown an increasing interest in developing their business in low- and middle-income countries, particularly very large countries like Brazil, China, and India. Smaller countries with narrower business opportunities may have more difficulty attracting these international companies. Reinsurers report that reinsurance capacity is available for crop and livestock programs that are properly designed and have rates that generate enough premium volume to cover the expected losses, operating costs, and costs of capital (including profits).

International reinsurance markets provide not only reinsurance capacity but also technical expertise. It is in the interest of reinsurers that an agricultural insurance program be properly designed and adequately priced, using international standards for underwriting, pricing, and loss adjustment.

Lack of Infrastructure

An important supply-side impediment to the provision of agricultural insurance in developing countries is the lack of infrastructure support. Agricultural insurance is highly data intensive. Individual grower yield-based crop insurance and indemnity products require individual farm-level yield data, which are costly to collect even in developed countries. Index-based insurance is also data intensive. Area-yield insurance programs, like the ones in Brazil or India, require aggregate yield data. In India aggregate data at the county level have been collected for more than 20 years by the local statistical departments (through crop-cutting experiments) to guide agricultural policy. However, the data are collected for policy not insurance purposes; for this reason, they do not usually include the cause of loss, which is important information for insurers. Likewise, weather-based crop insurance relies intensively on weather data and is dependent on the density of the weather station network and the quality and accuracy of the data collected.

The poor quality of data can also be an important impediment to the development of agricultural insurance. The data collection process should be transparent, subject to a strict protocol, and handled by a disinterested third party. Rainfall data have been collected for decades using manual rainfall gauges, which expose the data to erroneous reporting. Crop-yield surveys are not always conducted as they should be, usually because of lack of financial and human resources in statistical departments. Lack of historical data can prevent the proper modeling of the underlying risk, particularly the tail of the distribution, leading to the incorrect pricing of agricultural insurance products.

Agricultural risk assessment is complex, particularly regarding the impact of extreme natural events on crop and livestock losses. Catastrophe risk simulation techniques are powerful tools for assessing risk exposure at both the micro and macro levels. Such tools were initially developed to assess the catastrophic losses on the portfolio of property insurers. These tools are complex and costly to develop, making them unaffordable for most individual insurers, particularly in developing countries. The World Bank assisted the government of India in developing a probabilistic drought risk assessment model to assess the effects of different drought mitigation strategies and climate change scenarios. This model could also be used by agricultural insurers to assess the exposure of their insurance portfolio to drought (World Bank 2006). Governments could develop these models as public goods, providing domestic agricultural insurers with quantitative tools with which to better assess their agricultural risk exposure and design actuarially sound agricultural insurance products.

Agricultural insurance is expensive to service, particularly to small and marginal farmers scattered across the countryside. Private insurance companies usually do not have a network with which to reach these potential clients and are reluctant to invest in one given its high operational costs relative to the limited business opportunities. Delivery costs could be reduced by bundling agricultural insurance with other financial services, such as credit, and delivering it through rural banks, microfinance institutions, or input providers. The government could facilitate such delivery and in some cases provide subsidies to defray administrative and operational expenses.

Insurance companies in developing countries usually have very limited experience in agricultural insurance. The complexity of this line of business requires highly specialized skills. Start-up costs can be too high for private insurance companies to afford. In addition, innovations in insurance products developed by a leading company can be easily copied, making any return on such investments highly uncertain. Governments, with the assistance of the donor community, could provide technical assistance, possibly combined with some form of subsidies on start-up costs, to help insurers develop innovative and cost-effective agricultural insurance products. In Mexico, for example, the public reinsurance company (Agroasemex) provides technical assistance to farmers' self-insurance groups (Fondos).

Government has a role to play in offering public goods such as agricultural and weather databases and crop risk models. Supplying these public goods would provide domestic agricultural insurers with reliable data and quantitative tools with which to better assess their catastrophe risk exposure and design actuarially sound agricultural insurance products.

Low Risk Awareness

Farmers tend to be keenly aware of their production risks. In contrast, they tend to underestimate the likelihood or severity of catastrophic events. Stakeholder consultations in India and Mongolia suggest that farmers and herders recall the occurrence of major past events but tend to underestimate their severity. The U.S. Congress reported that insured producers tend to purchase too much insurance for relatively common events and too little insurance for low-probability events that are beyond their financial capacity (Wright and Hewitt 1994). Such behavior has been extensively discussed in the literature (see, for example, Kunreuther, Sanderson, and Vetschera 1985).

This tendency to underestimate catastrophic events may make farmers and herders unwilling to purchase agricultural insurance, particularly against extreme losses. Governments, in close collaboration with the insurance industry, could develop risk awareness campaigns to sensitize farmers and herders about their exposure to catastrophic events.

Lack of Insurance Culture

A commonly cited reason for the low demand for agricultural insurance in developing countries is the limited understanding of its benefits. Insurance is often perceived as a nonviable investment because premiums are collected every year but indemnities are paid much less frequently. The general population views insurance coverage as a privilege of the rich. This is particularly true for agricultural insurance, which, by definition, pays only when infrequent events occur.

Insurance is a complex financial product. Many rural households in developing nations are not financially literate, and insurance is an unfamiliar concept to many potential policyholders. As a result, the few insurance products that are currently available in low- and middle-income markets are not well understood by potential buyers. Policy exclusions and coverage limitations are often a source of confusion. Thus, potential buyers, even educated ones, sometimes prefer to retain risk than trust a third party like an insurance company.

In partnership with insurance companies and other stakeholders involved in agricultural risk management programs, governments can play a central role in promoting education campaigns and training for farmers on the role of agricultural insurance. Such activities would raise financial literacy among the rural community.

Lack of Affordability

Although the limited ability to pay cannot be considered, strictly speaking, a market imperfection, it contributes to the lack of demand for insurance and can be an equity rationale for public intervention. In most developing countries, low incomes inhibit the development of insurance markets. Incomes for the vast majority of the population are absorbed by basic necessities, such as food and housing. Where insurance is available, health insurance and life insurance are usually given higher priority over agricultural insurance.

A recent analysis indicates that there is very limited provision of insurance in the world's poorest countries, although there is some reason to believe that microinsurance penetration will increase in the future, particularly for life and health insurance (Roth, McCord, and Liber 2007). In many cases, rural households involved in agricultural activities do not generate enough profits to cover the costs of agricultural insurance.

Governments may want to provide premium subsidies as part of a social safety net program, targeting, for example, small and marginal farmers. These subsidies could be designed to provide farmers with financial incentives to engage in agricultural risk reduction activities.

Regulatory Impediments

The regulatory frameworks governing insurance markets in many low- and middle-income countries tend to be underdeveloped. As a result, short-term market incentives and regulatory constraints can in some cases inhibit increased penetration of insurance, including agricultural insurance.

In most countries, agricultural insurance is treated as part of the nonlife insurance business and therefore subject to the same regulatory requirements as, for example, automobile insurance. It is rarely mentioned in insurance law. For example, the insurance law for the Western African francophone countries, governed by the CIMA (Inter-African Conference on Insurance Markets) code, has only one article about agricultural insurance (Article 55).

Innovative agricultural insurance products, such as index-based crop insurance or parametric (weather-based) crop insurance, require an enabling regulatory framework. This new type of insurance, in which indemnity payments are based on an index (such as average yield in a given geographical area or rainfall levels) rather than actual individual losses, can challenge the basic requirements of insurable interest. Business interruption insurance covers firms experiencing insurable revenue losses that may not be associated with the loss of a physical asset. Formulating weather-based insurance as a special class of business interruption, which protects against losses and extra costs as a result of an insured event, may facilitate the regulation and supervision of weather-based insurance.

Another regulatory principle is that the insurance product indemnifies insured losses. This requirement aims at distinguishing insurance from other hedging instruments. A strict interpretation of this principle may exclude index-based products as an insurance product, because an index is used as a proxy for losses, which is by definition imperfectly correlated with the individual losses.

Governments can play an important role in promoting an enabling legal and regulatory framework. This framework should allow for the development of both traditional indemnity-based and innovative agricultural insurance products, such as index-based insurance; crowd in insurance and reinsurance companies; and protect farmers against potential insurers' malpractice (for example, nonpayment of valid claims).

Pricing and Subsidizing Agricultural Insurance

The above-mentioned market and regulatory imperfections affect the cost of agricultural insurance. Better understanding of the effect of these imperfections on the pricing of agricultural insurance products will help policymakers design public support programs aimed at reducing the cost of insurance.

Pricing agricultural insurance products is a critical stage in designing products that are attractive and affordable to farmers and herders and financially viable and sustainable for insurers. It requires a long series of high-quality historical agricultural/weather data. The price of agricultural insurance in competitive markets depends ultimately on the demand for and supply of insurance. Prices tend to increase when the demand exceeds the supply, and they tend to decrease when the supply of insurance exceeds the demand. However, the price of agricultural insurance (or insurance premium) is driven by some key factors, which can be identified by decomposing the technical insurance premium (table 2.1).

The annual expected loss, or pure premium, is based on the loss frequency and the loss severity of the underlying risk. Basic actuarial techniques should be used to price any insurance products, including agricultural (indemnity-based and index-based) products. Actuarial techniques currently used in most developing countries tend to price the insurance

Table 2.1 Technical Decomposition of Agriculture Insurance Premium

Premium component	Possible role of government
Catastrophe load	
Cost of risk capital	Act as reinsurer of last resort for top risk layers.
	Create conducive regulatory framework to attract reinsurers.
Uncertainty costs	Provide long time series of data.
Expense load	
Start-up cost	Provide technical assistance and public goods.
Underwriting costs	
Administrative costs	
Monitoring costs	Involve extension services.
Loss adjustment costs	
Marketing costs	Promote education and awareness campaigns.
Delivery costs	Promote alternative delivery channels, such as rural financial institutions and input providers.
Annual expected loss	
Loss frequency	Collect and manage agricultural and weather data.
Loss severity	Provide agricultural risk assessment models.

Source: Authors.

products on a stand-alone basis, using, for example, the normal theory method (see World Bank 2007b). This approach assumes that the underlying statistical distribution of the loss is normally distributed.

Another approach—the experience-based approach, based on the credibility theory—has recently been promoted in several countries, including India (World Bank 2007b). This approach does not impose a specific statistical distribution. Instead, it allows for the adjustment of the expected loss based on additional credible information (such as insured losses of other products). It is particularly relevant for (indemnity-based and index-based) crop insurance products that cover systemic risks. The credibility theory has also recently been applied to weather-based crop insurance products (Mahul, Clarke, and Verma 2009).

The expense load compensates the insurer for the administration and operating expenses of providing insurance, including start-up costs, which will be recovered (amortized) over a given period of time (for example, five years). These costs can be significant when a new line of insurance business is established, because the insurer needs to create an administrative apparatus, build a database, and develop new products. These costs are particularly high for index-based products, which require specific product development.

The insurer also faces operational expenses, such as underwriting, marketing, delivery, claims adjustment, and monitoring costs. These costs tend to be higher for agricultural insurance products, because they are technical products that require additional underwriting work, loss adjustment, and monitoring and because the delivery costs of reaching farmers, particularly small and marginal farmers in the countryside, are higher.

Start-up costs tend to be more expensive for index-based insurance products, whereas indemnity-based insurance usually generates higher underwriting costs and loss assessment costs. Partnerships with local institutions (such as local financial institutions or farmers groups or cooperatives) can help reduce these costs. In India, for example, self-help groups, under the insurer's supervision, handle some operational tasks of a livestock insurance program, including premium collection and loss adjustment of small claims. The Fondos in Mexico and the farmer (reclamation) groups in China also rely on their members to perform some insurance tasks on behalf of the insurer. Relying on insureds in this manner requires training and closely supervising them, but such models work relatively well in the long term, because both the insured and insurers have incentives to keep administrative and operating costs at a minimum.

The catastrophe load is the amount charged to compensate the insurer for bearing risk. In any given year, the actual loss can be much larger than the average loss. The catastrophe load tends to be relatively low (for example, 5 percent of premiums or less) for lines such as private passenger automobile insurance, where loss volatilities and correlations are low and exposure to catastrophic risk minimal. It is typically much higher in lines of insurance exposed to catastrophe loss, such as agricultural insurance, where the actual loss can be many times the expected loss. The insurer must secure enough risk capital to be able to ensure the timely payment of any major losses. To do so, it sets aside reserves or purchases reinsurance or other risk transfer instruments. The cost of risk capital includes the opportunity cost of holding reserves (for example, the spread between long-term and short-term interest rates) or the cost of risk transfer (for example, reinsurance premium). In addition, the insurer can add in a cost that reflects the uncertainty about the quality of the data used to price the insurance product.

The respective sizes of the three components of the technical insurance premium depend on the products and the markets. For example, named-peril crop insurance products, such as hail insurance, do not have a high catastrophe load, because these risks are usually localized and can be diversified. Loss assessment costs are also limited, because the losses caused by this peril are relatively easy to identify and quantify using crop percentage damage estimation procedures. In contrast, the systemic component of drought forces the insurers to charge high catastrophe loads, making such insurance expensive. Because it is a progressive peril whose impact can be measured only on actual production and yields, loss adjustment is more complex and costly. Index-based insurance is particularly well suited to insuring drought in crops, using rainfall deficit during the cropping season as the proxy for drought.

Public Subsidies to Agricultural Insurance

The government subsidizes the premium cost to farmers in many MPCI programs (see chapter 3). Such subsidies have rarely been applied to named-peril insurance products, such as hail insurance, partly because the costs of providing such insurance are usually low enough that farmers can afford to pay the premiums themselves.

Government subsidies are usually designed to increase insurance penetration by reducing the insurance premium charged to the policyholder. Such public subsidies may be justified by the existence of market imperfections, but there is a risk that public intervention distorts the price signals, crowds out the private sector, and generates unsustainable costs for the government.

In a well-functioning private insurance market, premiums should be risk based and differentiated so that each buyer pays a premium sufficient to cover his or her own expected loss and expense costs as well as a profit loading to compensate the insurer for bearing insurance risks. With risk-based premiums, buyers bear the full costs of their risk-generating activities and thus have incentives to engage in risk mitigation and not to overindulge in risky activities. Subsidized agricultural insurance induces overinvestment in risky areas. These adverse incentive effects increase the expected losses from catastrophes and impose costs on governments, taxpayers, and donors.

Many economists question the economic rationale for such premium subsidy programs. Siamwalla and Valdes (1986) identify a number of circumstances in which subsidies could be justified. These include situations in which the development of support capacity (specifically technology and information) can be shown to be a public (as opposed to a private) good; positive externalities are apparent (for example, farmers adopt less risk-averting practices that raise output over time); the decapitalization of small farms can be avoided; and intertemporal rural consumption can be stabilized on an efficient basis. Their argument is consistent with the growing literature on poverty traps (see, for example, Barnett, Barrett, and Skees 2007).

Governments usually justify premium subsidies based on their effect on demand, supply, and fiscal balances. On the demand side, they argue that farmers cannot afford to pay the high costs of comprehensive crop or livestock insurance coverage and that premium subsidies are therefore necessary to promote widespread adoption. On the supply side, they argue that premium subsidies act as an incentive for private commercial companies to enter this class of business, because the subsidies enable them to charge the high premiums required to cover expected losses and their high administrative and operating costs. From a fiscal viewpoint, they justify premium subsidies as a way of substituting government postdisaster compensation payments with formal ex ante crop insurance.

Two main types of insurance subsidies can be distinguished (Cummins and Mahul 2009). Market-enhancing insurance subsidies support the development of risk market infrastructure that enables competitive insurance markets. These subsidies focus on the development of public goods and technical assistance that enhance the risk market infrastructure and facilitate participation of the private insurance industry. Social insurance premium subsidies are provided by governments as part of social safety net or wealth transfer programs.

Market-Enhancing Subsidies

If an underlying failure of the insurance market exists, government intervention may enhance aggregate social welfare. The market-enhancing view recognizes that market failures can create suboptimal allocations of resources and that private sector coordination is not always effective. Public policy should facilitate the development of risk-market infrastructure that enables market-based solutions, such as the creation of public goods. Governments should avoid creating new, permanent government institutions that substitute for private solutions, although government institutions can be involved in very specific circumstances in which risks are ill defined and private market solutions not available (Cummins and Mahul 2009).

Market-enhancing insurance subsidies aim to create and support healthy and sustainable competition among insurance and reinsurance companies by reducing frictional costs, informational costs, and entry barriers. As discussed above, several market and regulatory imperfections can be corrected to create a competitive agricultural insurance market. The provision of public goods such as data sets, crop risk models, capacity building, and other types of technical assistance can contribute to the development of agricultural insurance. Financing of start-up costs through public subsidies can generate a social surplus. An enabling regulatory framework can allow insurers and reinsurers to develop innovative insurance products, such as index-based insurance.

Governments can also provide financial capacity by acting as reinsurers of last resort for the top risk layers, where both uncertainty and possible extreme losses make insurance very expensive or unavailable. For example, the Mexican public reinsurance company Agroasemex provides unlimited reinsurance (up to 100 percent of the total sum insured) to the Fondos; traditional private stop-loss reinsurance treaties are usually capped.

Market-enhancing subsidies reduce insurance premiums and therefore benefit farmers and herders. However, their impact may be difficult to quantify. Moreover, these indirect premium subsidies are not always visible to the farming community. Governments usually want to take actions that benefit potential electors in a more visible manner.

Social Insurance Premium Subsidies

Social insurance premium subsidies aim at transferring wealth to the farming community by reducing farmer-paid insurance premiums. Experience shows that this form of premium subsidy (a) is usually inefficient and increasingly expensive, because direct premium subsidies tend to be untargeted and available to all policyholders, whatever their ability to pay (because it is politically difficult to discriminate regarding the level of premium subsidies among the population); (b) remains permanent, even though the government introduces it as temporary; (c) represents an increasing fiscal burden for the government, because the eligibility criteria are relaxed or the subsidy levels increase; (d) mainly benefit policyholders in high-risk zones and large farmers (because the absolute premium subsidy usually increases with the total sum insured; only a few agricultural insurance programs, such as the Indian agricultural insurance scheme, provide special treatment to small and marginal farmers, such as specific premium subsidies [see chapter 3]). Social insurance premium subsidies can also create perverse behavioral incentives, because they distort the price signals sent through the premiums paid by farmers and hence induce them to make investment decisions, such as unsustainable production practices, that would not be optimal without such price distortions.

The most common type of direct premium subsidy is a proportional subsidy, whereby the government pays a fraction of the total premium. Such subsidies are available in most countries (see chapter 3). Premium subsidies can also be provided in excess of a capped premium, as they are in India. Farmers pay a flat premium rate—say, 3 percent—and the government pays the difference between the actuarially sound rate and the capped rate (see Cummins and Mahul 2009).

Insurance programs tend to be inefficient as wealth transfer programs (Wright and Hewitt 1994). However, when the public financial delivery systems face severe leakages and inefficiencies, as they do in many developing countries, private financial delivery systems may be more cost-effective in channeling financial assistance to poor households. In this case, social premium subsidies targeted to poor households may be justified as part of social safety net programs.

World Trade Organization Agreements and Agricultural Insurance Premium Subsidies

World Trade Organization (WTO) legislation has arguably had a major influence in promoting the spread of government-subsidized agricultural insurance since the Uruguay Round of multilateral trade negotiations in 1994, specifically by exempting agricultural insurance premium subsidies from the list of state aid and subsidies that have to be reduced or eliminated. The Uruguay Round agreements committed WTO members to the reduction of trade-distorting agricultural support, in particular the reduction in output price support measures and subsidies directly related to production quantities. In WTO terminology, government subsidies and other aids are identified by "boxes": green (permitted subsidies that do not distort trade), amber (subsidies to be reduced or phased out), and red (forbidden subsidies). There is also an intermediate blue box for subsidies that are tied to programs designed to limit production.

Government financial support to agricultural disaster relief or compensation payments and financing of agricultural insurance premium subsidies for insurance against natural disasters is permitted under WTO legislation where the government declares a natural disaster; farmers' losses must exceed 30 percent of average gross income or production in the past three years in order to be eligible for such payments. Agricultural premium subsidies are conceptually included under the green box. As private commercial insurance companies do not wait for governments to declare a disaster before making indemnity payments to insured crop and livestock producers, however, in practice most subsidies of agricultural insurance schemes in Europe and North America are amber box subsidies and must therefore be reduced after 2010.

European Union (EU) regulations for agriculture state that, with respect to adverse weather conditions that are deemed a natural disaster (for example, frost, hail, ice, rain, drought) for agricultural crops, qualifying losses must exceed 30 percent of normal production in all areas, and the maximum compensation cannot exceed 90 percent of the losses in less favorable areas (such as mountain areas) and 80 percent of the losses in other areas.[1] Where crop insurance is offered against adverse weather conditions, governments may subsidize up to 80 percent of the costs of insurance premiums. Natural disaster losses (losses caused by earthquakes, floods, or fire, for example) can be compensated at up to 100 percent of the loss, and up to 80 percent of the premium can be subsidized by the government. For losses caused by adverse climatic events or animal and plant diseases, compensation may be granted for up to 100 percent of actual costs; where insurance cover is provided against these perils, the maximum permitted subsidy is 50 percent of the cost of the premium. EU legislation permits aid of up to 100 percent for the removal of fallen stock (dead animals) and up to 75 percent for the destruction of carcasses.

WTO legislation has had two main effects. First, it has increased the levels of government premium subsidy support in countries that already provided subsidized crop insurance. This includes both the United States and the EU member states, which have some of the highest premium subsidy support levels anywhere in the world. In several European countries, average subsidy levels exceed 70 percent of the costs of premiums. Second, since 2000 it has led to the introduction of government-sponsored agricultural insurance premium subsidy programs in many countries, including Brazil, Chile, China, France, the Republic of Korea, Senegal, and Turkey. The features of these new subsidized agricultural insurance programs are analyzed in chapter 3.

Compulsory versus Voluntary Insurance

Premium subsidies are sometimes insufficient to induce farmers and herders to purchase agricultural insurance. In this case, governments may be tempted to make agricultural insurance compulsory in order to eliminate, or at least reduce, the need for recurrent postdisaster public intervention.

Compulsory insurance is sometimes suggested when farmers/herders underestimate the likelihood of catastrophic events and fail to adequately prepare for them (cognitive failure). It can also be suggested when economic agents do not fully internalize the financial consequences of their actions (for example, liability insurance). This argument is valid for all types of catastrophe risks. Compulsory property catastrophe insurance programs have been implemented in many developed and developing countries, including France, Romania, Turkey, and the United States.

Compulsory insurance is sometimes viewed as the response to adverse selection. Distorted insurance premium rates induce high-risk but not low-risk farmers to purchase insurance. The performance of the insurance program deteriorates as lower-risk farmers stay out of or leave the program, leading to its collapse. Compulsory insurance ensures that low-risk farmers participate in the program, forcing them to cross-subsidize high-risk farmers, thereby ensuring the viability of the program. However, this artificial viability may be socially suboptimal, as the aggregate loss of welfare of the low-risk farmers may exceed the aggregate welfare surplus of the high-risk farmers. The appropriate response to the problem of adverse selection is through an actuarially sound insurance program based on risk discrimination.

Compulsory insurance is sometimes invoked when a minimum participation is required to pool risks and cover fixed costs. The economic rationale of the pooling argument is somewhat questionable, because the basic concept of pooling relies on a group of homogeneous risks in which all participating agents will benefit from risk pooling. Compulsory insurance forces low-risk agents to participate in a scheme based on a wealth-transfer not a risk-pooling mechanism.

Several developing countries, including Honduras, India, and the Philippines, provide compulsory credit-linked crop insurance for borrowing farmers. These programs aim at transferring the farmers' default risk as a result of adverse natural events to the insurance industry, thus increasing the farmers' creditworthiness.

Climate Change

There is growing evidence that the frequency and severity of hydrometeorological events are on the rise, partly as a result of global warming. The Fourth Assessment Report by the International Panel for Climate Change (2007, p. 30) concludes that "warming of the climate system is unequivocal, as is now evident from observations of increases in global average air and ocean temperatures, widespread melting of snow and ice, and rising global mean sea level." The agricultural sector is particularly affected by more frequent and more severe adverse natural events, such as drought, floods, and windstorms, thus reinforcing the systemic component of the adverse natural events.

Insurance can potentially play an important role in climate change adaptation for households in developing countries as part of the overall climate change adaptation strategy. Market-based insurance premiums can signal the underlying risk exposure and help farmers and governments better assess and manage the economic impact of natural disasters. They can also provide farmers with incentives to adapt to climate change (for example, by shifting from crops that are unviable in the medium term as a result of climate change). However, any premium subsidy program that distorts the risk-based premiums may send the wrong economic incentives to farmers and impede, or at least delay, adaptation strategies.

Innovative catastrophe risk models are used to investigate the impact of climate change on the frequency and severity of catastrophe losses. A drought risk model was developed for Andhra Pradesh, India, to provide a robust analytical framework for simulating the long-term impact of drought in agriculture under several climate scenarios. It shows that global climate change is likely to increase the benefits of shifting from water-intensive crops like rice to drought-resistant crops in drought-prone districts (World Bank 2006). Seo and Mahul (2009) examine the impact of climate change on catastrophe hurricane risk models. They show that the recent 50-year period of climate change has potentially increased North Atlantic hurricane frequency by 30 percent. This increase in hurricane frequency is equivalent to an increase in risk to human property of less than 10 years' worth of U.S. coastal property growth.

In the case of drought, risk financing arrangements like insurance offer farmers a valuable opportunity to finance their losses, but they can perpetuate farmers' heavy dependence on rainfall. New financing products should provide an incentive to permanently switch to alternative, more sustainable, agricultural and economic practices, such as less water-intensive crops (particularly high-value cash crops), livestock, or some agroprocessing activities. Developing contingent financing schemes that could facilitate this transitional drought adaptation process appears to be an important area for further work (World Bank 2006).

Governments could support two lines of innovative financing products. Drought adaptation insurance could provide coverage against risks caused by a shift from nonviable farming to viable (agricultural and nonagricultural) businesses. This insurance product would protect farmers against new sources of risks resulting from a change to farming practices that are more drought resilient and less water intensive. Drought adaptation credit could provide initial capital to shift to a long-term viable business. In the event of an unexpected loss caused by a failure in the adaptation investment, repayments could be postponed or (partially) forgiven. These financial arrangements for drought adaptation would try to induce farmers to shift away from farming practices that are known to be unviable in the long term because of global climate change. These arrangements would offer farmers the opportunity to share new risks associated with the transition with society, because the adaptation process would benefit both farmers and society. With assistance from the World Bank, the government of India has piloted these drought adaptation strategies in selected communities in Andhra Pradesh. The programs have helped farmers shift from nonviable crops to livestock and designed livestock insurance policy for small ruminants for these communities.

The impact of climate change on the severity and frequency of extreme weather events may create additional incentives (or social pressure) for governments to intervene in agricultural insurance. Insurers and reinsurers may question the insurability of risks that become too frequent and limit their overall exposure to catastrophe losses. Governments may help agricultural producers further engage in agricultural risk mitigation to reduce recurrent losses and provide financial capacity to complement the risk capacity of the private insurance and reinsurance markets.

Modernizing the Agricultural Sector

Agricultural insurance can be an important tool for spurring rural economic development and the modernization of the agricultural sector, because it helps transfer excessive agricultural risks to a third party. This may be an important motivating factor for providing insurance in developing countries.

Increasing Access to Credit

The limited access to credit makes agricultural households particularly vulnerable to unexpected income shocks, such as adverse weather. They often reduce their income risk by diversifying and choosing low-risk activities or technology, which usually have low average returns.

Access to credit is severely restricted for a large part of the rural population, mainly because banks do not think that the economic and financial preconditions are met to expand their portfolio of agricultural loans. The main constraints include low population density and small average loans, which increase the transactions costs of financial intermediation, making it difficult for formal financial institutions to operate on a commercially viable basis. The seasonality of agricultural production and its exposure to natural disasters heighten the probability of default risk and expose financial institutions to covariant risks (in prices and yields).

Collateral requirements to minimize risk exposure by formal financial institutions can further hamper access to formal financial services. Most traditional lenders require land and buildings as collateral. Small farmers often lack assets that can be collateralized, or the value of their assets is substantially reduced by legal difficulties (such as lack of formal property titles). Microfinance, which provides access to credit without formal collateral, has opened access to loans for millions of poor people, but it has not reached most agricultural activities (World Bank 2008).

The perceived risk associated with agricultural lending, partly caused by production variability and price volatility, is one of the main reasons why commercial banks are reluctant to venture into agricultural lending. Techniques for identifying, assessing, and reducing risks could provide an incentive for commercial banks to exploit the market opportunities offered by demand for agricultural credit. This demand is expected to grow as producers move from subsistence farming, where no input credit is needed, to semicommercial and commercial farming, where productive investments (in hybrid seeds, fertilizers, and irrigation, for example) have to be made to ensure the financial viability of the business.

Loan defaults are driven by a number of risks, including not only production and price risks but also personal risks (for example, health). They can increase because of the culture of loan default that may lead some borrowers to avoid loan repayment even if they are able to repay a loan or to spend borrowed funds inappropriately (on consumption rather than investment, for example). In addition, the legal system may not be strong enough to follow up on loan defaulters.

Agricultural insurance can facilitate access to credit, because it increases the creditworthiness of farmers and other agents in the agricultural sector. To the extent that agricultural insurance contributes to the overall financial stability of the agribusiness sector, indirect benefits in terms of credit availability may be realized at other levels of the agribusiness marketing chain. Financial instability at the farm level arising from yield or price shocks may lead to instabilities at other levels of the processing and marketing chain. In this way, instruments that contribute to stability at the farm level may ease credit constraints for agents at other levels of the agribusiness complex. Government-sponsored agricultural programs in developing countries are usually linked to credit, as in India or Morocco.

In many developing countries, rural banks retain credit risk (partly caused by adverse natural events) on their books, acting de facto as insurers of last resort. These banking institutions are usually not equipped to retain these production risks, which can affect the viability of their overall lending activities. Agricultural insurance can assist governments in transferring these agricultural risks to third parties, such as insurance companies.

Facilitating the Adoption of Higher-Yielding Activities

Agricultural insurance can help farmers and herders invest in more profitable but sometimes riskier activities. Poor farmers in developing countries tend to adopt safety-first behavior, basing their production decisions on a survival strategy that minimizes the likelihood that their revenue will fall below a certain level (de Janvry, Fafchamps, and Sadoulet 1991). Agricultural insurance can help farmers invest in more profitable activities, because insurance contributes to the transfer of excess risk to a third party. Governments may want to promote this risk-transfer instrument as part of their overall policy on the modernization of agriculture.

In the context of climate change, insurance can also facilitate the adoption of adaptation activities. In India, for example, farmers in Andhra Pradesh were encouraged to shift from rainfed crops to livestock as a way to better mitigate the impact of recurrent droughts on their livelihood, and a livestock insurance policy was especially designed for those farmers (World Bank 2006).

Improving the Management of Postdisaster Assistance Programs

By their very nature, postdisaster assistance programs are unplanned and can expose the government to open-ended fiscal responsibility. Agricultural insurance programs can help governments better manage the budgetary impact of ad hoc assistance programs. Doing so is particularly relevant in developing countries, where any intervention in the agricultural sector can have a major impact on the government budget.

Actuarially sound premium rates reflect the true cost of risk (that is, the price of the underlying risk exposure of any agricultural business activity). Actuarially sound rating could help the government better forecast public financial support and better target farmers. It could also benefit farmers, because it allows for a more timely payment system and, ultimately, a more equitable crop insurance subsidy scheme (World Bank 2007b). In India, for example, the postdisaster financing of insured crop yield losses creates significant delays (of several months) in the claims settlement process. Agricultural insurance and related agricultural risk assessment techniques can allow the governments to better plan for probable major losses and secure immediate liquidity in the aftermath of a disaster.

Note

1. The regulations appear in EU Community Guideline OJC 28 (or OJ C232 of 2000) and in the new Commission Regulation (EC) No. 70/2001. After 2010 compensations for losses caused by adverse weather conditions must be reduced to 50 percent, except where farmers have taken out a crop insurance policy with a minimum coverage level of 50 percent of the normal crop production. This condition is very similar to that in the United States, where eligibility for federal disaster relief is conditional on the farmers having minimum catastrophe coverage under the Federal Crop Insurance Program.

CHAPTER 3

Comparative Analysis of Agriculture Insurance Programs

T his chapter presents the key results and findings of the 2008 World Bank survey of insurance companies, conducted in 65 countries. Appendix D presents more detailed results that identify individual countries. Case study information on each of the countries included in the survey is presented in appendix E, available in the Publications and Research section of the Web site http://www.insuranceforthepoor.org.

Survey Objectives and Methodology

The key objectives of the survey were to document international experience with public and private agricultural insurance in developed and developing economies and to examine the ways in which governments support agricultural insurance. The findings of the survey were used to make some recommendations for developing countries that plan to begin offering or to develop agricultural insurance (chapter 4).

The survey was based on a questionnaire designed by the World Bank to elicit information about the organizational structure of agricultural insurance in each country; the type of agricultural insurer (public or private); and, in markets with public sector intervention, the nature and types of support and their cost to the public sector. The study was also designed to allow for a simple comparison of the financial performance of private and public sector agricultural insurance programs.

Agricultural insurance covers crops, livestock (inclusive of poultry), forestry, and aquaculture. The focus of the survey was, however, on public support for crop and livestock insurance; the survey was not designed to provide detailed information on forestry or aquaculture insurance.

The questionnaire (see appendix C) contains the following sections:

- Agricultural insurance market structure by type of insurer (public, private commercial, private mutual, coinsurance pools)

- Agricultural reinsurance market structure and constraints to reinsurance access

- Types of agricultural insurance products and services offered by private and public insurers, including traditional indemnity-based products and new index-based products

- Types of public intervention and costs of these interventions during 2003–07

- Insurance uptake and penetration rates in 2003–07

- Insurance results for 2003–07

- A series of questions relating to natural disaster relief mechanisms.

The questionnaires were sent by e-mail to agricultural insurance companies in all 104 countries that were known to have some form of agricultural insurance provision in 2008. Sixty-five countries returned the questionnaire. The World Bank team supplemented these questionnaires with information drawn from third-party sources, including interviews and insurance company Web sites.[1] In most countries, respondents completed the questionnaires for the whole market; in Chile, India, and Portugal, the questionnaire applied only to the respondent's own insurance company. The survey included 65 countries (62 percent of all countries with agricultural insurance), including 21 high-income, 18 upper-middle-income, 20 lower-middle-income, and 6 low-income countries (table 3.1). As the main focus of this study is on agricultural insurance in developing

Table 3.1 Countries Covered by the World Bank Survey, by Development Status

Development status	Countries with agricultural insurance			Countries included in survey	Percentage of countries in group covered by survey
	Countries with agricultural insurance	Countries with pilot schemes	Total		
High-income countries	38	2	40	21	52
Middle- and low-income countries	48	16	64	44	69
Upper-middle-income countries	27	0	27	18	67
Lower-middle-income countries	17	8	25	20	80
Low-income countries	4	8	12	6	50
All countries	86	18	104	65	62

Source: World Bank Survey 2008.

countries, the very high proportion of responses received from respondents in low- and middle-income countries makes the survey highly representative of and informative about the agricultural insurance market in developing countries.

As the map indicates, the survey includes a high percentage of countries in North America, Central and South America, Western Europe, Southeast Asia, and Australasia (figure 3.1). It includes fewer countries in the Middle East and Central Asia and only a handful of countries in Sub-Saharan Africa, mainly because agricultural insurance is underdeveloped there.[2]

Origins of and Trends in the Provision of Agricultural Insurance

The origins of agricultural insurance can be traced to the late 17th century in Western Europe with the formation by farmers of private mutual crop hail insurance companies and livestock insurance mutual companies. Private mutual crop hail insurance spread to the United States, Canada, and Argentina in the late 19th century and early 20th century. One of the earliest examples of public sector multiple peril crop insurance (MPCI) is the U.S. Federal Crop Insurance Program (FCIP), introduced by the Roosevelt Administration in the 1930s in response to major droughts, with the key objective of stabilizing farm incomes.

Figure 3.1 Countries Covered by the World Bank Survey on Agricultural Insurance

Agricultural insurance

Reviewed under World Bank Survey (2008)

This map was produced by the
Map Design Unit of The World Bank.
The boundaries, colors, denominations
and any other information shown on
this map do not imply, on the part of
The World Bank Group, any judgment
on the legal status of any territory, or
any endorsement or acceptance of
such boundaries.

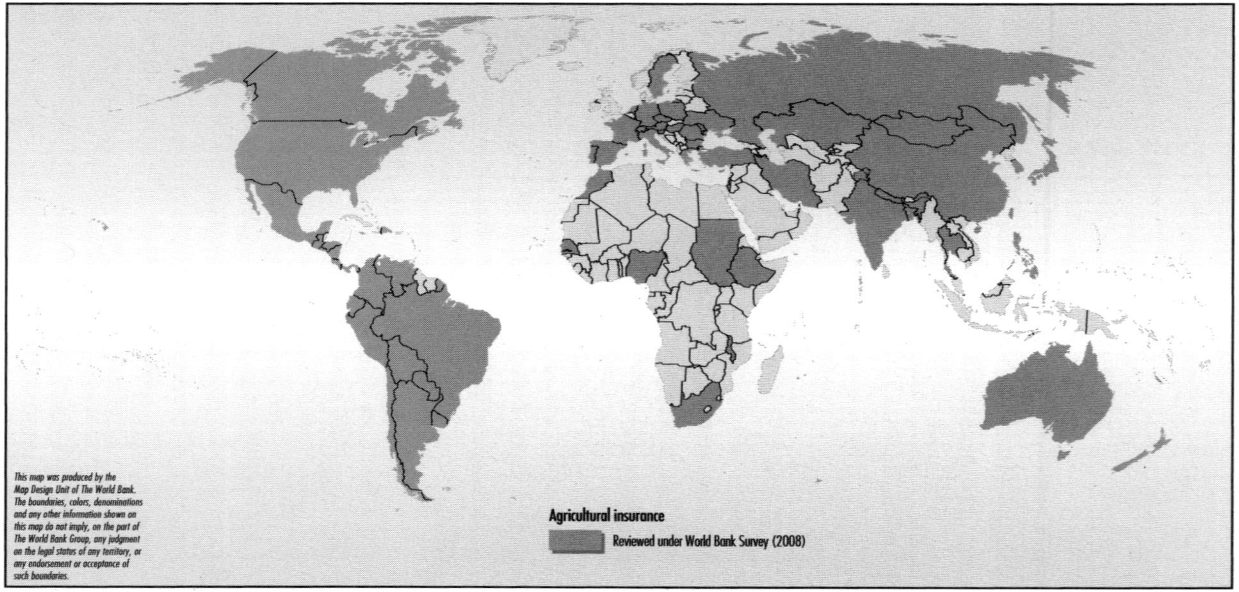

Source: World Bank Survey 2008.

Between the 1950s and the end of the 1980s, there was a major growth in public sector MPCI in Latin America (Brazil, Costa Rica, Ecuador, Mexico, and République Bolivariana de Venezuela) and Asia (India and the Philippines), often linked to seasonal production credit programs for small farmers. In Western Europe national programs for subsidized MPCI were introduced in Portugal and Spain in 1980. In the former Soviet Union, public sector MPCI was implemented on state farms. Many of these public sector programs had high operating costs and very high loss ratios, which were exacerbated by the levying of very low premium rates and poor management. In Latin America, most public sector programs were terminated by 1990 because of their poor results. In India, the Philippines, Portugal, Spain, and the United States, various measures were introduced to strengthen and reform national programs.

Historically, many government-subsidized MPCI programs have performed very poorly, with excessively high administration costs and claims well in excess of the premiums collected from farmers (table 3.2). In order to assess the full economic costs of these government-subsidized programs, Hazell (1992) presented his analysis in terms of the ratio of paid indemnities to the nonsubsidized portion of the premium (P) paid by the farmer, termed the *producer loss ratio* (I/P). This measure is distinct from a conventional or gross loss ratio, which is calculated as the ratio of paid indemnities to total original gross premiums. Administrative and

Table 3.2 Financial Performance of Subsidized Multiple Peril Crop Insurance Programs

Country	Period	I/P (indemnity/ premium paid by producer)	A/P (administration cost/premium paid by producer)	(I + A)/P (indemnity + administration costs/ premium paid by producer)
Brazil (PROAGRO)	1975–81	4.29	0.28	4.57
Costa Rica (INS)	1970–89	2.26	0.54	2.80
India (CCIS)	1985–89	5.11	—	—
Japan	1947–77	1.48	1.17	2.60
(agriculture)	1985–89	0.99	3.57	4.56
Mexico (ANAGSA)	1980–89	3.18	0.47	3.65
Philippines (PCIC)	1981–89	3.94	1.80	5.74
United States (FCIP)	1980–89	1.87	0.55	2.42

Source: Hazell 1992.
Note: — = Not available.

organizational costs (A/P) and the ratio ($I + A$)/P in table 3.2 are presented using the producer premium as the denominator.[3]

Hazell's (1992) analysis shows that for every dollar in collected premiums paid by producers, the paid indemnities (value of claims) and administrative costs on these programs ranged from $2.40 (in the United States) to $5.70 (in the Philippines). An ($I + A$)/P ratio of more than 1.0 indicates that a program is not collecting adequate premiums from the insured producer to cover indemnities and administrative costs. The programs in table 3.2 relied heavily on government financial subsidies (of premiums, claims, or administration expenses) to remain in operation. The programs in Brazil and Mexico were eventually terminated because of insolvency; the other subsidized programs remain in operation.

Since the 1990s, the trend has been for governments to promote agricultural insurance through the private insurance sector, often backed by government financial support (public-private partnerships [PPPs]). Following the break-up of the Soviet Union in 1990, many of the state-owned monopoly agricultural insurers in Eastern Europe were privatized, and markets were opened up to competition by new private commercial companies providing crop and livestock insurance policies. In the United States, the FCIP's MPCI program is implemented through 17 private insurers or managing general agents. In Latin America, new private commercial agricultural insurance was introduced in Brazil, Chile, and Ecuador during the last decade.

In some countries, such as Spain, the government has also replaced ad hoc natural disaster compensation programs with ex ante formal crop and livestock insurance programs implemented by the private insurance sector and promoted and supported by the government through provision of premium subsidies or reinsurance protection. In other countries, such as the United States, the government continues to provide public sector disaster relief in addition to highly subsidized crop insurance.

Global Agricultural Insurance Markets

The private insurance industry is involved, in various forms, in agricultural insurance programs in most countries. Agricultural insurance is provided exclusively by the private sector (most commonly private limited companies but also by private mutual, cooperative, and microfinance institution insurers) in 54 percent of all countries surveyed. It is provided only by the public sector in 9 percent of countries (Costa Rica, Cyprus, the Islamic Republic of Iran, Israel, Mauritius, and Nigeria). In 37 percent of surveyed countries, both the public and the private sectors are involved in agricultural insurance (table 3.3). (Information on individual countries appears in appendix D.)

The majority of the surveyed countries (82 percent of total) offer both crop and livestock insurance. Ten countries (15 percent of total) offer only crop insurance; two countries (Bangladesh and Mongolia) offer only livestock insurance.

Public versus Private Institutional Frameworks

The survey encompasses a wide range of organizational structures for agricultural crop insurance (table 3.4). The least common structure is a public sector model under which a national or parastatal insurance company is responsible for underwriting insurance, usually backed by public sector reinsurance arrangements. This model was found in very few countries. One example is the Indian National Agricultural Insurance Scheme (NAIS), which is implemented through the public sector Agricultural Insurance Company of India (AICI), whose losses in excess of premiums are covered by the federal and state governments on a 50:50 basis.[4] Other public sector crop insurance models include those in Canada, Cyprus, Greece, Iran, and the Philippines.

The private sector model, under which commercial insurers are exclusively responsible for underwriting crop and livestock insurance, backed by private reinsurance, is identified in slightly more than half of the 65 surveyed countries. This is the dominant system in 62 percent of countries in Europe and 70 percent in Latin America and the Caribbean. The largest private sector agricultural insurance markets include the private crop hail program in the United States, which carries no premium subsidies, and a program in Argentina in which a group of 29 commercial and mutual insurance companies compete to underwrite crop hail and a smaller volume of MPCI, forestry, livestock, and aquaculture business.

Table 3.3 Public and Private Providers of Agricultural Insurance, by Development Status and Region (percent, except where otherwise indicated)

Development status/region	Number of countries	Private	Public	Public-private partnerships	Coinsurance pools	Crop insurance only	Livestock insurance only	Crop and livestock insurance
Development Status								
High-income	21	62	10	29	5	5	0	95
Upper-middle-income	18	61	11	28	11	17	0	83
Lower-middle-income	20	55	5	40	20	30	5	65
Low-income	6	0	17	83	17	0	17	83
All countries	65	54	9	37	12	15	3	82
Region								
Africa	8	25	25	50	13	13	0	88
Asia	12	25	17	58	25	8	17	75
Europe	21	62	5	33	14	5	0	95
Latin America and the Caribbean	20	70	5	25	5	35	0	65
North America	2	50	0	50	0	0	0	100
Oceania	2	100	0	0	0	0	0	100
All countries	65	54	9	37	12	15	3	82

Source: World Bank Survey 2008.

Table 3.4 Public-Private Institutional Frameworks in Agricultural Insurance

Type of model	Features	Examples
Public sector insurance	Entity usually operates as the sole or monopoly insurer in the country. The government is the main or exclusive reinsurer.	• Canada: 10 provincial government crop insurance corporations, which are partly reinsured by the federal government • Cyprus: one national insurer, the Agricultural Insurance Organization of the Ministry of Agriculture • Greece: one government entity, the Hellenic Agricultural Insurance Organization (ELGA) • India: the National Agricultural Insurance Scheme (NAIS), implemented by the public agricultural crop insurance company, the Agricultural Insurance Company of India (AICI) • Iran: one insurer, the government-owned Agricultural Insurance Fund • Philippines: one national insurer for crop and livestock insurance, the Philippines Crop Insurance Corporation (PCIC)
Private sector insurance with no government support	Private commercial or mutual insurance companies (either general non–life insurance companies or specialist agricultural insurers) actively compete for business and purchase proportional and nonproportional reinsurance from international commercial reinsurers.	• Argentina: 29 private commercial and mutual insurers, mainly crop hail insurers • South Africa: 7 private commercial and mutual companies and underwriting agencies offering crop insurance, livestock insurance, or both • Australia: 15 private companies underwriting crop insurance, livestock insurance, or both • Others: Germany, Hungary, the Netherlands, Sweden, New Zealand

(continued)

Table 3.4 Public-Private Institutional Frameworks in Agricultural Insurance (*continued*)

Type of model	Features	Examples
Public–Private Partnerships		
National agricultural insurance schemes with monopoly agricultural insurer	A national subsidized private sector crop and livestock insurance is implemented through a single entity offering standard policy forms and uniform rating structure; this entity is responsible for loss adjustment. Model involves high levels of government premium subsidy support and support for reinsurance.	• Private coinsurance pools: Agroseguro (Spain); Tarsim Pool (Turkey) • Single national insurer: National Agriculture Cooperative Federation cooperative crop and livestock insurer (Republic of Korea)
Commercial competition with high level of control	Individual commercial insurers compete for business, but policy design and premium rating criteria are controlled by the government, and insurers may be obligated to offer crop insurance to all farmer types and regions in order to order to qualify for premium subsidies.	• Portugal: SIPAC crop insurance scheme, underwritten by about 15 private general insurance companies • United States: FCIP/MPCI program, implemented by 17 private companies/managing agents
Commercial competition with lower level of control	Private companies are free to elect which crops and regions and perils they underwrite and the premium rates they charge. The main role of the government is to subsidize premiums.	• Brazil, Chile, France, Italy, Mexico, Poland, Russian Federation

Source: Authors.

Australia, France (crop hail), Germany (crop hail and livestock), New Zealand, South Africa, and Sweden also follow this model. Most of these private agricultural insurance markets offer named-peril crop insurance.

Under the PPP model, agricultural insurance is implemented by the private sector with assistance from government, usually in the form of premium subsidies but also often through reinsurance. The most comprehensive PPP arrangements are found under the national agricultural insurance schemes in Spain and Turkey; in both countries, monopoly private coinsurance pools are authorized to implement subsidized agricultural insurance nationally, backed by public and private sector reinsurance. The Republic of Korea also has a single national cooperative insurer, which acts as the sole provider of crop and livestock insurance, with major government support in the form of premium subsidies, administrative and operating (A&O) expense subsidies, and reinsurance subsidies. Another PPP model involves individual private sector commercial insurers that compete for business but that may have to comply with strict insurance policy design and rating criteria in order to qualify for public sector premium subsidies. Examples include the FCIP in the United States and the Portuguese government–sponsored System for the Protection of Climatic Risks (SIPAC) crop insurance program. In other countries, PPPs operate under a looser partnership, in which the government's main role is to act as a passive provider of agricultural insurance premium subsidies or reinsurance support to private commercial insurers. Such models are in place in Brazil, Chile, France (increasingly through subsidized MPCI), Italy, and Mexico.

Coinsurance Pools in Agricultural Insurance

Coinsurance pools are found in nine countries. The most notable example is Spain, where the national combined agrarian insurance scheme is underwritten by Agroseguro for a coinsurance pool of 21 private commercial insurers, 7 mutual insurance companies, and the national catastrophe reinsurer. Other countries with coinsurance pools include Austria; China, where coinsurance pools led by the People's Insurance Company of China underwrite crop, livestock, forestry, and aquaculture risks in several provinces, including Zhenjiang and Hainan; Malawi, which has a weather index crop insurance pool; Mongolia, which has a livestock insurance indemnity pool; and Turkey, where the Tarsim Pool was created in 2006 to underwrite subsidized crop and livestock insurance (table 3.5; see also appendix E). There are major cost advantages of pool arrangements (box 3.1). Programs are managed either by the lead insurer or by an agency appointed by the pool.

Table 3.5 Countries with Agricultural Coinsurance Pool Arrangements

Country	Year established	Description
Argentina	2005	Mendoza Province Fruits and Vineyard Hail Crop Insurance Scheme is led by Sancor and La Segunda, under a pool coinsurance arrangement with several other local private commercial insurance companies. Crop insurance market in Argentina is active and competitive.
Austria	1947	Austrian Hail Insurance Company, a mutual with 17 founding companies, is sole provider of crop hail insurance.
China	2006	Two agricultural insurance coinsurance pool schemes are led by the People's Insurance Company of China (PICC), one in Zeijiang Province (crops, livestock, forestry, and aquaculture), the other in Hainan Province (crops, forestry, livestock). PICC acts as the scheme administrator and loss adjuster on behalf of coinsurers.
Malawi	2006	Weather-based crop insurance underwritten by a pool of domestic insurance companies, coordinated by the association of insurers, is being piloted.
Mongolia	2006	Four private insurers offer livestock index mortality insurance through the Livestock Insurance Indemnity Pool, a public-private coinsurance pool.
Philippines	1978	A public-private coinsurance pool for livestock insurance is underwritten by the Government Service Insurance System (GSIS) and the Philippine Livestock Management Services Corporation (PLMSC), which has 14 participating coinsurers. There is one other crop and livestock insurer in the Philippines (PICC).
Spain	1980	Agroseguro, the largest public-private agricultural coinsurance pool in the world, is a specialist agricultural managing underwriting company formed by coinsurers to implement the Spanish national agricultural insurance scheme on their behalf. In 2008 Agroseguro comprised 28 private insurance company shareholders, 6 mutual insurer members, and the national reinsurer, Consorcio de Compensacion de Seguros. The largest shareholder and coinsurer is Mapfre Insurance Company, with a 30 percent share in the pool. There are no other agricultural insurance schemes in Spain, although some voluntary forestry and aquaculture insurance is written outside the national pool scheme.

(continued)

Table 3.5 Countries with Agricultural Coinsurance Pool Arrangements *(continued)*

Country	Year established	Description
Turkey	2006	Tarsim Agricultural Insurance Pool is a specialist insurance company formed by 16 private commercial companies, each with a 6.25 percent share in the company. Tarsim underwrites crop and livestock on the behalf of coinsurers. No other companies offer agricultural insurance in Turkey.
Ukraine	2000	Two crop coinsurance pool schemes are in operation. A large number of competing companies offer crop and livestock insurance.

Source: Authors.

Box 3.1 Benefits and Limitations of Coinsurance Pool Arrangements

Coinsurance pool arrangements have both benefits and limitations. Among the potential benefits, they achieve economies of scale by operating as a single entity with shared (pooled) administration and operating functions. This leads to costs savings from reduced staffing requirements (fixed costs), shared costs of product research and development (actuarial and rating), and reduced costs of underwriting and claims control and loss adjustment. Purchasing common account (pooled) reinsurance protection (rather than requiring individual companies to put in place their own reinsurance programs) leads to stronger negotiating position with reinsurers, larger and more balanced portfolios and better diversification of risk, reduced costs of reinsurance because of pooled risk exposure, and reduced transaction costs (such as reinsurance brokerage).

Under such an arrangement, there is therefore no competition on pricing, because most pools operate as monopolies (this is the case, for example, in Austria, Spain, and Turkey). The pool manager can ensure that common and high standards are maintained in the underwriting of crop and livestock insurance and in the adjusting of claims. Where companies are competing against one another for standard crop insurance business, there is often a problem of varying loss adjustment standards between companies.

Pool monopoly arrangements also have some limitations. These include the lack of market competition, resulting in limited range of products and services offered; the restricted range of perils insured; and the lack of price competition.

Source: Authors.

Size of Agricultural Insurance Markets and Premium Volume

The volume of global agricultural insurance premium has grown significantly since 2003, fueled by three main factors:

- Major increases in commodity prices and corresponding increases in the sum insured value of crops and livestock and the premiums generated

- The major expansion of agricultural insurance in emerging markets such as Brazil, China, and Eastern Europe

- The increase in government premium subsidy support for agricultural insurance in key countries, which has led to increased insurance uptake in many countries, including Brazil, China, Korea, Turkey, and the United States.

In 2003–05 the global agricultural insurance premium volume was estimated at about $7–$8 billion (Kasten 2005; Guy Carpenter 2006). This figure had risen to about 16.5 billion ($21 billion) by 2008 (Paris Re 2008).[5]

The global agricultural insurance premium volume for the 65 countries responding to the World Bank survey is estimated at $15.1 billion in 2007. It is divided into crop premiums of $13.5 billion (90 percent of total) and livestock premiums of $1.6 billion (10 percent of total). Agricultural insurance is highly concentrated in the 21 high-income countries, whose premium volume was $11.9 billion (86 percent of the total), equivalent to an average of 2.34 percent of 2007 agricultural GDP in these countries. In contrast, agricultural insurance accounts for only 0.29 percent of GDP in upper-middle-income countries and just 0.16 percent of GDP in lower-middle-income; in the six lower-income countries, it represented less than 0.01 percent of GDP (table 3.6).

North America accounts for 64 percent ($9.6 billion) of 2007 global agricultural insurance premiums, followed by Europe (17 percent), Asia (15 percent), Latin America and the Caribbean (3 percent), Oceania (0.7 percent), and Africa (0.4 percent). Except in South Africa, there is almost no tradition of agricultural insurance provision in Africa, which is very underdeveloped in terms of both crop and livestock insurance.

Table 3.6 Estimated Agricultural Insurance Premiums in 2007, by Development Status and Region

Development status/region	Number of countries	Estimated crop premium ($ million)	Estimated livestock premium ($ million)	Estimated agricultural premium ($ million)	Share of global agricultural premium	Agriculture insurance penetration (premium as percentage of 2007 agricultural GDP)
Development Status						
High-income	21	11,869.0	1,192.3	13,061.3	86.48	2.34
Upper-middle-income	18	872.6	40.1	912.7	6.04	0.29
Lower-middle-income	20	789.3	334.1	1,123.5	7.44	0.16
Low-income	6	0.2	4.8	5.0	0.03	0.00
All countries	65	13,531.1	1,571.4	15,102.4	100.00	0.92
Region						
Africa	8	58.5	5.0	63.5	0.42	0.13
Asia	12	1,265.9	1,047.1	2,313.0	15.32	0.31
Europe	21	2,102.6	434.8	2,537.4	16.80	0.64
Latin America and the Caribbean	20	461.3	26.3	487.6	3.23	0.24
North America	2	9,597.2	3.2	9,600.4	63.57	5.01
Oceania	2	45.6	54.9	100.5	0.67	0.38
All countries	65	13,531.1	1,571.4	15,102.4	100.00	0.92

Source: World Bank Survey 2008

The provision of agricultural insurance is highly concentrated in the top 10 countries ranked by 2007 premium volume, most of which are high-income economies (table 3.7). The United States dominates global agricultural insurance. It offers two very large crop insurance programs, FCIP, which provides subsidized MPCI, and a private commercial nonsubsidized crop hail program, as well as a much smaller livestock insurance program. Together these programs account for 56 percent of total global agricultural insurance premium volume and 5.2 percent of agricultural GDP in the United States. Other large providers of agricultural insurance include (in order of importance) Japan, Canada, Spain, and China. In 2007 China was ranked fifth by premium volume; on the basis of 2008 premium estimates of $1.75 billion, it jumped to second place (Air Worldwide 2009).

Subsidization of premiums is a key feature of most of the top 10 agricultural insurance markets. In the United States, premium subsidies amounted to $3.8 billion (58 percent of FCIP net premiums and 48 percent

Table 3.7 Estimated Agricultural Insurance Premium Volume in Top 10 Countries, 2007

Country	Number of crop and livestock insurance companies	Level of government premium subsidies	Estimated 2007 agricultural insurance premiums ($ million)	Percentage of total global premium volume	Agriculture insurance penetration (premium as percentage of 2007 agricultural GDP)
United States[a]	17	Very high	8,511	56.4	5.2
Japan	300	Very high	1,111	7.4	1.8
Canada	59	High	1,090	7.2	4.1
Spain	1	High	809	5.4	1.6
China	9	High	682	4.5	0.2
Italy	28	High	383	2.5	0.9
France	14	Restricted	366	2.4	0.6
Russian Federation[b]	69	High	315	2.1	0.6
Iran, Islamic Rep. of	1	Very high	241	1.6	0.8
Argentina	33	Very restricted	240	1.6	1.0
Total Top 10			13,746	91.0	1.6

Source: World Bank Survey 2008.
[a] Original gross premiums for crops insured under FCIP in 2007 are estimated at $8.02 billion, made up of $6.56 billion in technical premiums (net premium comprising producer premiums and premium subsidies) and $1.46 billion in A&O expense subsidies. In 2007 private crop hail premiums amounted to another $488 million. Livestock insurance premium was $3.2 million.
[b] No details were available as to the number of livestock insurers or the level of livestock premiums.

of estimated total original gross premiums) in 2007. In Iran premium subsidies amounted to 69 percent of total premiums.

In France livestock insurance and most crop hail business is not subsidized (premiums for some tree fruit and vegetables are subsidized, as is MPCI, which has received a 35 percent premium subsidy since 2005). In Argentina a private sector crop hail market has been unsubsidized for nearly 100 years, and only a few crops (for example, tobacco and wine grapes) are subsidized by local provincial governments.

Agricultural Crop and Livestock Insurance Products

Individual grower crop insurance products can be classified into two major groups: traditional indemnity-based products and index-based products (table 3.8).

Indemnity-based crop insurance products. Indemnity-based crop insurance products fall into two categories: (a) damage-based indemnity policies, which include hail insurance and named-peril crop insurance (known as *combined insurance* in Europe), and (b) yield-based indemnity products, which include MPCI yield shortfall cover and crop revenue insurance, which combines protection against both loss of physical crop yield and loss of market price.

Individual grower named-peril crop insurance is the most common product, offered in 69 percent of the 65 surveyed countries (table 3.9). Named-peril (mainly hail alone or with additional named perils) crop insurance is offered in all of the high-income countries. In contrast, just 45 percent of lower-middle-income countries and 50 percent of low-income countries offer named-peril crop insurance products. These differences reflect the fact that most high-income countries are located in the temperate regions of the world (Europe, North America, and Oceania) and face an appreciable hail and frost exposure, which is suited to named-peril insurance. Hail is not a key peril in the subtropics and tropics.

Yield-based MPCI is the second-most popular product, marketed in 63 percent of the surveyed countries. This product is available in less than half of all high-income countries; it is not available in Oceania. Individual grower MPCI is much more widely underwritten in upper-middle-income countries (72 percent) and lower-middle-income countries (85 percent),

Table 3.8 Indemnity- and Index-Based Crop Insurance Products

Type of insurance	Description
Traditional Crop Insurance	
Damage-based indemnity insurance (named-peril crop insurance)	Insurance in which the claim is calculated by measuring the percentage damage in the field soon after damage occurs. This figure, less a deductible expressed as a percentage, is applied to the preagreed sum insured, which may be based on production costs or expected crop revenue. Where damage cannot be measured accurately immediately after the loss, the assessment may be deferred until later in the crop season. Damage-based indemnity insurance is best known for hail but is also used for other named-peril insurance products, including frost, excessive rainfall, and wind.
Yield-based crop insurance (MPCI)	Insurance in which an insured yield (for example, tons/hectare) is established as a percentage of the historical average yield of the insured farmer. The insured yield is typically 50–70 percent of the average yield on the farm. If the realized yield is less than the insured yield, an indemnity is paid equal to the difference between the actual yield and the insured yield, multiplied by a preagreed value of sum insured per unit of yield. Yield-based crop insurance typically protects against multiple perils (many different causes of yield loss), because it is generally difficult to determine the exact cause of the loss.
Crop revenue insurance	Insurance that combines conventional loss crop yield–based MPCI insurance with protection against loss of market price at the time of sale of the crop. As of 2009, this product was marketed on a commercial basis only in the United States for grains and oilseeds with future contracts quoted on the Chicago Board of Trade.
Greenhouse insurance	Insurance that combines coverage of material damage to greenhouse structures and equipment and conventional crop insurance (usually restricted to named perils) to the covered greenhouse crop.

| Forestry insurance | Traditional damage-based indemnity insurance against fire and allied peril losses in standing timber. The valuation for insurance and indemnity purposes is often based on the investment and maintenance costs up to the point at which the trees can be harvested for timber, after which the value is based on the commercial value of the standing timber. |

Index-based Crop Insurance

Area-yield index insurance	Insurance in which the indemnity is based on the realized (harvested) average yield of an area such as a county or district. The insured yield is established as a percentage of the average yield for the area (typically 50–90 percent of the area average yield). An indemnity is paid if the realized average yield for the area is less than the insured yield, regardless of the actual yield on a policyholder's farm. This type of index insurance requires historical area yield data on which the normal average yield and insured yield can be established.
Weather index insurance	Insurance in which the indemnity is based on realizations of a specific weather parameter measured over a prespecified period of time at a particular weather station. The insurance can be structured to protect against index realizations that are either so high or so low that they are expected to cause crop losses. An indemnity is paid whenever the realized value of the index exceeds or falls short of a pre-specified threshold. The indemnity is calculated based on a preagreed sum insured per unit of the index (for example, dollars/millimeter of rainfall).
Normalized difference vegetation index/satellite insurance	Indexes constructed using time-series remote sensing imagery (for example, applications of false color infrared waveband to pasture index insurance, where the payout is based on a normalized difference vegetation index, which relates moisture deficit to pasture degradation). Research is being conducted on applications of synthetic aperture radar to crop flood insurance.

Source: Authors.

Table 3.9 Availability of Indemnity- and Index-Based Insurance, by Development Status and Region (percent, except where otherwise indicated)

Development status/region	Number of countries	Traditional indemnity-based					Index-based		
		Named peril	MPCI	Crop revenue	Crop greenhouse	Forestry	Area yield	Weather	Normalized dry vegetative index/satellite
Development Status									
High-income	21	100	48	5	62	48	10	10	14
Upper-middle-income	18	67	72	0	33	56	11	17	6
Lower-middle-income	20	45	85	5	25	20	25	35	10
Low-income	6	50	17	0	17	33	17	33	0
Region									
Africa	8	50	50	0	13	50	25	38	0
Asia	12	58	58	8	25	25	17	25	17
Europe	21	95	48	0	62	29	5	0	5
Latin America and the Caribbean	20	50	90	0	25	50	15	30	5
North America	2	100	100	50	50	50	100	100	100
Oceania	2	100	0	0	100	100	0	0	0
All countries	65	69	63	3	38	40	15	22	9

Source: World Bank Survey 2008.

especially in Latin America and the Caribbean (90 percent of surveyed countries). More than half of all responding countries in Asia, including China, Iran, Kazakhstan, and the Philippines, offer this product.

South Africa is the only country with unsubsidized MPCI. MPCI has yet to take off in the small number of lower-income countries surveyed: Ethiopia, which has a small pilot MPCI program, is the only low-income country offering MPCI.

Although yield shortfall indemnity, such as MPCI, has been taken up more widely in recent years, many programs that have adopted this method have had serious difficulties implementing it, because of poor insurance rating, lack of objective loss assessment, and inadequate design criteria to reduce the potential for moral hazard. (The performance of these schemes is reviewed later in this chapter.)

Greenhouse insurance is widely available in 38 percent of the respondent countries, including 62 percent of high-income countries; it is particularly widespread in Europe. A quarter of all countries in Asia and Latin America and the Caribbean offer this product.

Given the very restricted reinsurance market for standing timber fire cover, it is surprising that 40 percent of all countries offer this product. In most cases, however, the market is restricted to small numbers of specific risks, which are placed with international reinsurers on a facultative basis. The largest markets for forestry insurance are in Chile, Oceania, and Scandinavia. Canada offers no commercial standing timber cover. In the United States, this cover is underwritten only on a limited basis, under agency agreements with international markets.

Index-based crop insurance products. Crop index insurance includes three main types of product:

- Area-yield index insurance, which was first developed in Sweden in the early 1950s and which has been implemented on a national scale in India since 1979 and in the United States since 1993

- Crop weather index insurance, which has been commercially underwritten since 2002

- Normalized difference vegetation index/satellite index insurance, which has been applied to pasture in a few countries.

In 2007 area-yield index insurance was available in nine countries (15 percent of total), including, in order of the size of the program, India, where some 20 million farmers are insured under the NAIS program each year; the United States, Canada, Mexico, Morocco, Iran, and Ukraine; and, most recently, Peru and Senegal, which have pilot programs. This type of insurance has both advantages and disadvantages (table 3.10).

Crop weather index insurance is available in 14 (22 percent) of the surveyed countries, mainly on a pilot basis. This product is being piloted in low-income countries in Africa, Asia, and Central America (box 3.2). Adoption of the product is surprisingly high, given that the first weather index policy was underwritten only in 2002 (under the BASIX-ICICI Lombard scheme for rainfall deficit for groundnuts farmers in India).

Table 3.10 Advantages and Disadvantages of Area-Yield Index Crop Insurance

Advantages	Disadvantages
Adverse selection and moral hazard are minimized. The indemnity is based on average area yields, not individual farmers' yields. Individual farmers cannot therefore influence the yield outcome.	The occurrence of basis risk depends on the extent to which individual farmers' yield outcomes are positively correlated with the area-yield index.
Time-series county or district-level area-yield data are usually available in most countries.	Area-yield insurance will not work in areas with high losses because of localized perils, such as hail or localized frost pockets.
The policy acts as an all-risk yield shortfall guarantee policy; it is best suited to situations in which severe systemic risk (for example, drought) has a similar impact over the insured unit (for example, a district or county).	Area-yield insurance works best in a homogeneous climatic zone and where cropping systems for the insured crop are uniform (for example, same varieties, planting dates, management practices).
There is no need to conduct preinspections on individual farms or to collect individual grower yield data.	Methods of yield measurement and reporting may not be accurate, raising doubts about historical area yields.
There is no requirement to assess individual grower in-field area losses, which is very time-consuming and costly.	Sampling error and enumerator bias can be a major problem in determining average area yields.
The combination of reduced exposure to yield loss and reduced administrative costs offers the potential for lower premiums than those on individual farmer MPCI.	Farmers often have to wait three to six months postharvest for the official results of area yields to be published and indemnities to be paid if applicable.

Source: Authors, based on World Bank 2007a.

Box 3.2 The World Bank's Experience with Agricultural Index-Based Insurance

Since the late 1990s, the development of agricultural risk-modeling techniques and the emergence of insurance pools and index-based insurance have contributed to a revisiting of the potential role of agriculture insurance in emerging economies. The World Bank has provided technical assistance for the development of innovative agriculture insurance programs in both low- and middle-income countries, often tying these programs into agricultural finance support efforts and complementary efforts in agricultural extension. In particular, the World Bank has assisted several of its member countries in developing or enhancing index-based insurance products.

The interest in using index-based agricultural insurance has grown in recent years, particularly with respect to addressing the systemic component of agricultural production losses (such as those caused by a widespread drought). Index-based insurance offers several advantages over traditional insurance relying on individual losses, including lower monitoring costs and more transparent indemnity structure. However, this type of insurance faces some challenges (such as basis risk), which makes it cost-effective only for specific crops, perils, and geographical areas.

The implementation of index-based insurance in agriculture is relatively new. A number of projects have been piloted in low-income countries. As of 2009, more than 15 index-based agricultural insurance programs had been implemented or enhanced with World Bank assistance in low- and middle-income countries.

Mongolia has been piloting an index-based livestock product since 2005. Insurance indemnity payments are based on estimates of livestock mortality rates in local administrative areas from January through May, as estimated by the annual livestock census. This is the first time ever such a livestock index has been used for insurance purpose.

The World Bank has assisted the government of India in improving the National Agricultural Insurance Scheme (NAIS), which offers coverage against crop yield losses, using an area-yield index in the indemnity payment schedule. About 20 million farmers have been insured under this program, for a total liability of $7 billion, making this the largest crop insurance program in the world in terms of insured farmers. The World Bank Group has provided the government of India with technical assistance to move this scheme to an actuarial regime, in order to make it

(continued)

Box 3.2 *(continued)*

more attractive to farmers and reduce the fiscal exposure of the government. Area-yield crop insurance has recently been investigated in Bangladesh and Senegal.

The World Bank has provided technical assistance for the development of weather-based crop insurance products. It has assisted the government of India in developing the Weather-Based Crop Insurance Scheme (WBCIS). This scheme protects farmers against specific adverse natural events (rainfall deficiency, excess rainfall, low temperature) through weather-based insurance. More than 400,000 farmers purchased weather-based crop insurance in 2008. This program draws on small-scale weather-based insurance pilot programs conducted in India with World Bank technical assistance since 2003.

Weather-based crop insurance has been piloted in Malawi since 2005 (see box 3.3). During the 2008/09 season, about 2,600 farmers were covered, with a sum insured of $2.5 million. Weather risk programs have also been developed in Guatemala, Honduras, and Nicaragua (although only the program in Nicaragua, where 2,500 hectares of export crops with a value of $41.6 million were insured in 2008, is currently operational). In Thailand weather-based crop insurance is being offered on a pilot basis to 400 farmers for a total sum insured of $300,000. Other excess/deficit rainfall projects are under development in Ethiopia, Kenya, and Senegal, and the feasibility of other applications of index-based insurance is being assessed in Bangladesh, Burkina Faso, Indonesia, and Jamaica. These weather-based crop insurance pilots are linked to agricultural lending. They aim to strengthen agricultural finance, agricultural supply chains, and profitability in agriculture.

Some success has been observed in the pilot implementation of index-based crop insurance and particularly weather-based crop insurance. One of the main challenges in the future will be to scale up these pilot programs and develop risk market infrastructures that ensure the sustainability of these programs, mainly through PPPs.

Source: Authors, based on World Bank 2008a.

Commercial mainstream programs are operating only in Canada, India, Mexico, and the United States; use of the product is still at the pilot-testing stage in other countries, including China, Ethiopia, Guatemala, Honduras, Malawi, Nicaragua, Peru, and Thailand.

Crop weather index insurance for individual farmers has been pilot tested in Malawi with various crops, including maize and tobacco, as part of a bundled program involving input supply and credit (box 3.3). Normalized difference vegetation index/satellite index insurance is available for pasture in Canada, Iran, Mexico, Spain, and the United States. India has been piloting this technology for field crops.

Box 3.3 Weather Index–Based Crop Insurance in Malawi

At the beginning of 2005, the World Bank began work on a pilot program in Malawi to determine if index-based weather insurance would be a useful tool for managing agricultural risk. Traditional multiple peril crop insurance had been tried unsuccessfully on a small scale in Malawi, and Malawian insurers were both apprehensive about offering agricultural insurance and interested in seeing how an alternative to traditional multiple peril coverage would work.

Discussions were held with various groups to determine how and with whom this pilot project should be carried out. Immediate interest was shown by the National Association of Small Farmers (NASFAM), which works with farmers to develop marketing channels for value-added goods and encourages its member farmers, who are organized in clubs of 15–20 members, to invest in higher-return activities. NASFAM attributes the low productivity of Malawian farmers to both the lack of access to credit and the low quality of inputs. It saw potential for this product to be introduced for a number of crops in Malawi. For the first year, it choose groundnut as a pilot crop, because of its susceptibility to drought and its growth potential in Malawi.

Malawi's groundnut farmers had little access to the credit needed to purchase groundnut seed. They therefore traditionally relied on local seed, if any, for production. Many NASFAM farmers had shown interest in planting certified groundnut seed in order to improve revenues. Certified seed, which is more expensive than local seed, has a number of benefits, such as a higher resistance to fungal infections, which can destroy a crop. In addition, certified seed can be marketed as a named variety of groundnut seed rather than a generic version.

A three-phase weather-based crop insurance contract was designed in close collaboration with farmers' groups, domestic insurers, and international reinsurers. These contracts were initially offered in the four pilot areas.

(continued)

Box 3.3 *(continued)*

Because these weather contracts could mitigate the weather risk associated with lending to farmers, two banks, Opportunity International Bank of Malawi (OIBM) and Malawi Rural Finance Corporation (MRFC), agreed to lend farmers the money necessary to purchase certified seed if the farmers bought weather insurance.

In 2006, 892 groundnut farmers purchased weather-based crop insurance policies, for a total sum insured of $36,600. In 2008 the pilot was expanded to cash crops; 2,600 farmers bought these policies, for a total sum insured of $2.5 million.

The number of participants increased significantly in 2008. One of the main constraints is the poor density of the weather station network in Malawi. The World Bank is assisting the government in increasing the number of weather stations.

Source: World Bank 2009.

Livestock insurance products. Livestock insurance products include traditional animal accident and mortality cover as well as an epidemic disease cover and a livestock index mortality product. Named-peril accident and mortality insurance for individual animals is the basic traditional product for insuring livestock. Cover includes death caused by natural perils, such as fire, flood, lightning, and electrocution; it normally excludes diseases, specifically epidemic diseases.[6] Premiums are set based on normal mortality rates within the permitted age range, plus risk and administrative margins. They are generally expensive. As mortality is to a considerable extent influenced by management, the product suffers from adverse selection by the highest-risk farmers.

Herd insurance is a variation on individual animal mortality cover for larger herds. This product includes a deductible, which is borne by the policyholder before an indemnity is paid.

A few countries, most notably Germany, offer epidemic disease insurance. Insurance of government-ordered slaughter or quarantine is normally excluded. Epidemic disease insurance carries major and infrequent catastrophic claim exposures, necessitating a high reliance on reinsurance for risk transfer. Because of the difficulties of modeling epidemic disease spread and financial exposures, it is difficult to develop this type of insurance and to obtain support from international reinsurers.

Index insurance for livestock has been applied for mortality risk in Mongolia, where there is a high correlation between livestock losses and an "indexable" extreme weather parameter (that is, low temperature). Satellite imagery and normalized difference vegetation indexes are used for some pasture and rangeland products in Canada, Spain, and the United States.

Two-thirds of surveyed countries provide livestock accident and mortality cover, and 38 percent provide epidemic disease cover (table 3.11). Livestock mutual insurance has a 300-year history in Europe; it is not therefore surprising that it has the highest proportion of countries with standard mortality cover and epidemic disease cover for livestock. Although a high proportion of respondents reported that livestock epidemic disease insurance is available, this market is highly controlled by a

Table 3.11 Availability of Livestock Insurance, by Development Status and Region (percent, except where otherwise indicated)

Development status and region	Number of countries	Traditional indemnity insurance			Index-based insurance	
		Accident and mortality	Epidemic disease	Aquaculture	Mortality index	Other livestock insurance
Development Status						
High-income	22	77	55	45	0	14
Upper-middle-income	17	76	24	29	0	0
Lower-middle-income	20	55	30	20	5	0
Low-income	6	67	50	17	0	50
Region						
Africa	8	88	50	13	0	13
Asia	12	58	42	42	8	17
Europe	22	82	50	45	0	14
Latin America and the Caribbean	19	53	21	16	0	0
North America	2	100	0	0	0	0
Oceania	2	50	50	50	0	0
All countries	65	69	38	31	2	9

Source: World Bank Survey 2008.

few specialized international reinsurers, and local coverage is likely to be very restricted. Germany has one of the largest livestock insurance markets against epidemic diseases.

Livestock insurance is available in 55 percent of lower-middle-income and 67 percent of low-income countries. Many of the programs are small.

The other category of livestock insurance—found in half of all low-income countries—includes livestock microfinance or credit guarantee products, which guarantee the repayment of a loan in the event the animal dies before the loan is repaid. This type of product is available in Bangladesh and Nepal.

Aquaculture insurance—including off-shore marine and on-shore freshwater aquaculture insurance for fish stock, crustaceans, and shellfish—is reported as a separate class of livestock insurance. It is available in about a third of all countries surveyed. The largest markets for aquaculture insurance are in Southeast Asia, Chile, Canada, and Norway (Norway was not included in the survey).

There is only one livestock mortality index insurance scheme in the world. It is being piloted in Mongolia, under a public-private pool arrangement (box 3.4).

Delivery channels. In the developed insurance markets in high-income and upper-middle-income countries, insurance is traditionally marketed through insurance agents or brokers. Lower-income countries have large numbers of small and marginal crop and livestock producers. Developing low-cost delivery channels for marketing and administering agricultural insurance in these countries is a major challenge.

Countries use a variety of distribution channels for crop insurance and livestock insurance (table 3.12). In Europe insurance companies sell crop insurance policies through sales agents or cooperatives, which are particularly important in marketing crop hail insurance. In Asia sales agents and brokers play a much smaller role in marketing crop insurance; the two main channels are cooperatives/producer associations and banks/microfinance institutions. In Latin America and the Caribbean, brokers play the leading role in marketing insurance to farmers, followed by banks/microfinance institutions. In Africa none of the responding companies/countries identified sales through the rural

Box 3.4 Index-Based Livestock Insurance in Mongolia

In 2005 the government of Mongolia asked the World Bank for technical assistance in the design and implementation of a pilot program for index-based livestock insurance in order to protect herders against major livestock losses caused by harsh winters. The request recognized that smaller, individual livestock mortality risks are better addressed through appropriate household-level risk mitigation strategies.

The product created combines a commercial insurance product (the base insurance product) and a social product (the disaster response product). The base insurance product pays when livestock mortality rates in the local administrative area (*soum*) exceed 6 percent; losses beyond 30 percent are managed by the disaster response product. Payments are based on estimates of livestock mortality rates in *soums* from January through May, as estimated by the annual livestock census and, in the future, by a midyear livestock survey. This is the first time an index insurance product has been used in Mongolia, where traditional indemnity-based livestock insurance proved unsustainable given the extensive herding practices.

The program is offered through the Livestock Indemnity Insurance Pool (LIIP), a public-private risk-pooling arrangement, in which participating insurers share underwriting gains and losses based on the share of herder premium they bring into the pool. The LIIP is protected with a stop-loss reinsurance treaty, currently underwritten by the government and backed by a World Bank credit.

The LIIP has several major advantages:

- It fully insulates this line of business from other lines of insurance (an important feature given the limited capital of the insurance industry in Mongolia, which is still in its infancy).
- It fully secures the payment of indemnities, thereby eliminating any risk of default on payments.
- It allows insurance companies to pool their livestock insurance portfolio in different regions, which allows them to take advantage of the risk diversification benefits.
- It facilitates the capacity building of participating insurers.

The risk financing structure of the LIIP follows best practices. Insurance companies retain some portion of the risk, pool risk with other companies, and access public reinsurance for excess losses. It is expected that

(continued)

Box 3.4 *(continued)*

international reinsurers will provide capacity for the first reinsurance layers, with the government covering only catastrophic risk layers.

The first sales season started in 2006. As of 2009, the program was being piloted in four provinces (Bayankhongor, Khentii, Sukhbaatar, and Uvs), and four insurance companies were participating. The number of policies sold reached 2,400 in 2006, more than 3,700 policies in 2007, and 4,100 in 2008, representing 14 percent of herders in the pilot provinces. In mid-August 2008, following high livestock losses, $340,000 was paid out to 1,783 herders. All financing systems worked as planned; a small amount was drawn from the contingent debt facility.

Lenders have already started offering lower interest rates and better terms for loans to insured herders. Linking index-based livestock insurance to herder loans will be an important next step in reducing delivery costs.

Source: Authors, based on Mahul and Skees 2007.

Table 3.12 Main Sales Delivery Channels for Crop Insurance, by Development Status and Region (percent, except where otherwise indicated)

Development status/region	Number of countries	Insurer's own agents	Insurance brokers	Banks/ microfinance institutions	Cooperatives/ producer associations
Development Status					
High-income	21	52	10	5	33
Upper-middle-income	18	44	22	11	22
Lower-middle-income	19	47	16	32	5
Low-income	4	25	25	0	50
All countries	62	47	16	15	23
Region					
Africa	7	43	29	0	29
Asia	10	30	0	30	40
Europe	21	71	0	5	24
Latin America and the Caribbean	20	30	30	25	15
North America	2	100	0	0	0
Oceania	2	0	100	0	0
All countries	62	47	16	15	23

Source: World Bank Survey 2008.

banking sector, although there have been some attempts to deliver weather-based crop insurance through microfinance institutions (in Senegal and Tanzania, for example).

For livestock insurance, a much higher proportion (62 percent) of countries report that their main sales channel is insurance company sales agents (in Europe 90 percent of sales are through company agents). In Asia the two main distribution channels for livestock insurance are insurance company agents and cooperative associations. In Latin America and the Caribbean the proportion of sales made through insurance companies is higher for livestock than crop insurance. In Africa 50 percent of livestock insurance is sold through insurance company sales agents; banks and cooperatives also play an important role in distributing products.

In developing countries, where rural insurance company infrastructure is often lacking, there may be opportunities to market agricultural insurance through rural banking networks. Agricultural lending banks and microfinance institutions are already involved in assessing small farmers' creditworthiness and loan disbursements, and they have the distribution network to administer large numbers of small borrowers. These institutions could offer credit-linked crop insurance. Among the surveyed countries, one-third of lower-middle-income countries report that their main distribution channel is through banks and microfinance institutions (table 3.13). This distribution channel is well developed in Asia. In contrast, Africa has yet to develop linkages between banking and agricultural insurance. In settings in which the number of small farms is large, affiliation with a bank may be the most cost-effective route to providing agricultural insurance.

In a number of insurance programs operated by centralized marketing organizations, premiums are deducted at the source (that is, the organization deducts crop insurance premiums from the sales revenue owed to farmers and directly pays the premiums to the insurer), communication with member farmers is quick and easy, and payments of indemnity are made quickly. Examples of such schemes include the Wincrop banana windstorm insurance scheme for small-scale export banana producers in the Windward Islands (Dominica, Grenada, St. Lucia, and St. Vincent and the Grenadines) and the Mauritius Sugar Insurance Fund. Insurance programs linked to contract farming also exist in India and Kenya.

Table 3.13 Main Sales Delivery Channels for Livestock Insurance, by Development Status and Region (percent, except where otherwise indicated)

Development status/region	Number of countries	Insurer's own agents	Insurance brokers	Banks and/or microfinance institutions	Cooperatives/ producer associations
Development Status					
High-income	20	65	15	0	20
Upper-middle-income	13	54	23	8	15
Lower-middle-income	14	79	0	7	14
Low income	6	33	17	17	33
Region					
Africa	8	50	13	13	25
Asia	9	44	11	0	44
Europe	20	90	5	0	5
Latin America and the Caribbean	12	55	18	9	18
North America	2	50	0	0	50
Oceania	2	0	100	0	0
All countries	53	62	13	6	19

Source: World Bank Survey 2008.

Compulsory versus Voluntary Insurance

In many countries, third-party liability insurance for automobiles is mandatory and bank loans, including mortgages, are often conditional on the borrower purchasing life insurance to protect the loan. As discussed in chapter 2, the justification for compulsory insurance in agriculture centers on two arguments. First, mandatory coverage allows the insurer to mitigate adverse selection. Second, it enables underwriters to achieve a viable portfolio size and a balanced spread of risk and to reduce administrative costs per insured. Many new voluntary crop insurance programs suffer from low uptake in early years and never achieve a balanced spread of risk.

Agricultural insurance is voluntary in 78 percent of the surveyed countries; it is compulsory for either crop or livestock in 13 percent. It is compulsory (conditionally required) for borrowers of seasonal crop production credit or livestock investment loans in 11 percent of surveyed countries (table 3.14).

Table 3.14 Nature of Agricultural Insurance (Voluntary versus Compulsory), by Development Status and Region (percent, except where otherwise indicated)

Development status/region	Number of countries	Voluntary	Compulsory	Compulsory for borrowers of credit
Development Status				
High-income[a]	20	80	20	0
Upper-middle-income	18	83	17	0
Lower-middle-income	20	70	5	25
Low-income	6	67	0	33
Region				
Africa	8	75	13	13
Asia	11	36	27	36
Europe[a]	21	86	14	0
Latin America and the Caribbean	20	85	5	10
North America	2	100	0	0
Oceania	2	100	0	0
All countries	64	77	13	11

Source: World Bank Survey 2008.
[a] Excludes Israel, for which data were not available.

Agricultural insurance is compulsory in China, Cyprus, Japan, Kazakhstan, Mauritius, the Netherlands, Switzerland, and the Windward Islands (table 3.15). China introduced compulsory subsidized epidemic disease cover in swine in 2007. Cyprus has a government compulsory insurance scheme for all crops. Japan's subsidized rice insurance has been compulsory for many years. In Kazakhstan crop insurance is compulsory but livestock insurance is voluntary. In Mauritius growers with more than 0.04 hectares of sugarcane are required to insure against fire, windstorm, drought, excess rain, and yellow spot disease. In the Netherlands and Switzerland, epidemic disease insurance in livestock is compulsory for all livestock owners. In the Windward Islands, export banana growers are required to carry windstorm cover.

Another seven countries (11 percent), all lower-middle-income or low-income countries, make crop or livestock insurance a condition for credit recipients. These countries include Bangladesh, Ecuador, Honduras, India, Morocco, Nepal, and the Philippines.

Table 3.15 Countries with Compulsory Crop or Livestock Insurance

Country	Crop insurance	Livestock insurance	Comment
High-income Countries			
Japan	Compulsory	Voluntary	Compulsory for main agricultural products (wheat, barley, and rice for farmers whose farms are larger than 0.3 hectares). Voluntary for livestock, fruits, fruit trees, and greenhouse insurance.
Netherlands	Voluntary	Compulsory for epidemic disease	
Switzerland	Voluntary	Compulsory for epidemic disease	
Upper-middle-income Countries			
China	Voluntary	Compulsory for epidemic disease in sows (swine)	Following major swine losses in 2007 from porcine reproductive and respiratory disease (PRRD), the government introduced a compulsory subsidized national PRRD disease insurance program for sows.
Mauritius	Compulsory	n.a.	The Sugar Cane Act makes windstorm insurance mandatory for all sugar cane growers with more than 0.04 hectares of sugarcane.
Windward Islands (Dominica, Grenada, St. Lucia, and St. Vincent and the Grenadines)	Compulsory	n.a.	Windstorm cover for export bananas is compulsory in Dominica and St. Vincent. In St. Lucia banana insurance is voluntary.
Lower-middle-income Countries			
Ecuador	Voluntary/compulsory	Voluntary	Crop insurance is compulsory for small and marginal farmers who access public sector seasonal crop loans. Livestock insurance is completely voluntary.
Honduras	Voluntary/compulsory	Voluntary	In general, agricultural insurance purchase is voluntary. However, the state- owned bank, Banadesa, requires collateral and/or insurance for loans to the agricultural sector.

India	Voluntary/compulsory	Voluntary	Public sector crop insurance through the Agricultural Insurance Company of India is compulsory for all farmers who access seasonal crop production credit from the lending institutions; it is voluntary for farmers who do not borrow. Private sector crop weather index insurance offered is purely voluntary.
Morocco	Voluntary/compulsory	Voluntary	Drought insurance program from the Mutuelle Agricole Marocaine d'Assurances is compulsory for borrowing farmers. Hail, fire, and livestock insurance are voluntary.
Philippines	Voluntary/compulsory	Voluntary	The majority of formal seasonal credit for rice and corn production is through the Land Bank of the Philippines, which requires borrowers to insure. However, 18 percent of rice premiums and 21 percent of corn premiums (in 2005/06) came from nonborrowing farmers. Livestock insurance is voluntary, although financial institutions lending for livestock production may require that insurance is taken out.
Low-income Countries			
Bangladesh	No crop insurance	Voluntary/compulsory	Some microfinance institutions have introduced compulsory livestock mortality insurance for microcredit loans for livestock.
Nepal	Voluntary	Voluntary/compulsory	Livestock insurance is compulsory for farmers wishing to access livestock investment loans from rural development banks and the country's sole microfinance institution. The cooperatives link livestock loans and livestock insurance, although this is not mandatory in most cases.

Source: Authors, based on World Bank Survey 2008.
Note: n.a. = Not applicable.

Agricultural Reinsurance

Agricultural reinsurance provides insurance to agricultural insurers. This access to additional risk capital is critical, because agricultural risks can be systemic and create major losses. Without reinsurance, insurers may not be able to meet the demand for agricultural insurance or may be exposed to default risk.

Agricultural reinsurance protection is purchased exclusively from private commercial reinsurers in two-thirds of the surveyed countries (table 3.16; see also appendix C). The agricultural reinsurance market is dominated by a small group of global reinsurers that specialize in agricultural reinsurance, including Munich Re, Swiss Re, Paris Re, Hannover Re, Mapfre Re, Partner Re, Scor, and several Bermudan reinsurers, as well as various syndicates at Lloyd's, which tend to specialize in bloodstock (high-value racehorses and reproductive animals), livestock, and aquaculture.[7] Reinsurers provide both proportional quota share treaty and nonproportional treaty reinsurance for crops, livestock, forestry, and aquaculture.

Table 3.16 Availability of Agricultural Reinsurance, by Development Status and Region (percent, except where otherwise indicated)

Development status/region	Number of countries	Private commercial reinsurance	Government reinsurance	Public and private reinsurance	No reinsurance
Development Status					
High-income	21	57	10	33	0
Upper-middle-income	18	67	11	22	0
Lower-middle-income	20	75	10	15	0
Low-income	6	67	0	0	33
Region					
Africa	8	88	0	12	0
Asia	11	18	36	28	18
Europe	22	68	5	27	0
Latin America and the Caribbean	20	85	5	10	0
North America	2	0	0	100	0
Oceania	2	100	0	0	0
All countries	65	66	9	22	3

Source: World Bank Survey 2008.

Agricultural reinsurance is provided through PPP in 22 percent of the surveyed countries (table 3.17). Public-private reinsurance is available in one-third of all high-income countries, in 15 percent of middle-income countries, and in no low-income countries. The government provides major reinsurance support to agriculture in both Canada and the United States. In Europe the public sector plays a very important role in agricultural reinsurance, either in the form of public sector reinsurers (Spain and Turkey) or through arrangements with government to settle part of the excess claims (Israel, Italy, Poland, and Portugal). Public sector reinsurers play a very important role in several upper-middle-income countries. These institutions include the Instituto Nacional de Resseguro do Brasil; Agroasemex, the specialist parastatal agricultural reinsurer, in Mexico; and Milli Re in Turkey. Three lower-middle-income countries also have important public-private reinsurance arrangements. In India the government plays a very important role in providing free stop-loss protection to the Agricultural Insurance Company of India under the National Agricultural Insurance Scheme (NAIS). The Indian weather-based crop insurance programs offered by the public and private sectors are, however, 100 percent reinsured on a commercial basis with reinsurers, including the General Insurance Corporation of India and international reinsurers. In China the national reinsurer China Re provides support to local insurers, and local governments are acting as coreinsurers on a stop-loss basis in some provinces.

In 6 of the 65 surveyed countries (Costa Rica, Cyprus, Iran, Japan, Kazakhstan, and Mongolia), agricultural reinsurance is provided exclusively by the government. In two countries (Bangladesh and Nepal)—where agricultural insurance is restricted to very small livestock insurance schemes, which are implemented mainly through cooperatives, communities, or microfinance institutions—there is no reinsurance protection for these programs.

In India, Portugal, and Spain, the government plays an important role in reinsurance provision. In India the federal government and state governments settle (on a 50:50 basis) any losses on the NAIS that exceed a 100 percent loss ratio for food crops and a 150 percent loss ratio for commercial and horticultural crops (figure 3.2). This program is provided free of cost (no premium is charged) by government to the implementing

Table 3.17 Public-Private Agricultural Reinsurance Programs

Country	Government reinsurer	Description
High-income Countries		
Canada	Federal government	The federal government reinsures five provinces with stop-loss reinsurance. Most provinces purchase private international stop-loss reinsurance.
Israel	Government	Kanat, the main agricultural insurer, purchases stop-loss reinsurance from both the government and international reinsurers.
Italy	Government	The government provides crop hail and MPCI reinsurance on both a quota share and stop-loss treaty basis. Private international reinsurers support the crop hail business on a nonproportional basis.
Korea, Republic of	Government stop loss	Program reinsures 100 percent of losses in excess of 180 percent of gross net premium income. Local insurers provide quota share reinsurance of national agricultural insurance scheme and then retrocede part of their liability to international reinsurers on a proportional or nonproportional basis.
Portugal	System for the Protection of Climatic Risks (SIPAC), government stop loss	Local insurers may elect to reinsure with international reinsurers or the government crop stop-loss fund, which reinsures 85 percent of losses in excess of 65 percent of gross net premium income (GNPI) in Region E, 80 percent in Region D, and 120 percent GNPI in regions A, B, C.
Spain	National catastrophe reinsurer	Since 1980 Consorcio de Compensacion de Seguros has provided layered stop-loss reinsurance protection for Agroseguro's viable lines and excess of loss reinsurance on experimental lines.
United States	Standard reinsurance agreement of the federal government	Using the standard reinsurance agreement, the 14 insurance companies underwriting MPCI business may reinsure their programs with the federal government under very favorable terms. Some companies purchase additional private commercial stop-loss reinsurance.

Upper-middle-income Countries

Brazil	National reinsurer (Instituto Nacional de Resseguro do Brasil) and government stop-loss fund (Fundo de Estabilidade do Seguro Rural)	Until 2007, the Brazilian Reinsurance Institute had monopoly control over all reinsurance in Brazil. It provided quota share protection to local insurers and then retroceded a large share to specialist international reinsurers.
Mexico	National agricultural reinsurer (Agroasemex)	Agroasemex provides reinsurance to the private commercial crop and livestock insurers; it reinsures the Fondos' small farmer crop and livestock programs as well as various parametric crop index programs for state governments.
Poland	Government reinsurance fund for drought	The government reinsures drought losses. All other perils, as well as crop and livestock programs, are reinsured with international reinsurers.
Turkey	National reinsurer (Milli Re)	The Tarsim crop and livestock pool program is reinsured by Milli Re and international reinsurers, led by Munich Re.

Lower-middle-income Countries

China	National reinsurer (China Re) plus provincial government funding of excess losses	Until 2005, Chinese insurers were required to make cessions to China Re. These compulsory cessions have been phased out, and companies are now free to reinsure with China Re or private international reinsurers. Nearly all international reinsurance is placed on a stop-loss treaty basis. Various provincial governments are also providing coreinsurance support for high-level catastrophe loss layers.
India	National Reinsurer (General Insurance Corporation of India) for commercial weather index insurance; the government for the National Area-Based Crop Insurance scheme (NAIS)	Crop weather index insurance is reinsured on a commercial basis with compulsory quota share cessions to the General Insurance Corporation of India and international reinsurers. NAIS is protected on a stop-loss basis by the government.
Morocco	Government	Under the Mutuelle Agricole Marocaine d'Assurances drought insurance scheme for various crops, the government retains a primary layer and excess layers are reinsured by international reinsurers.

Source: Authors, based on World Bank Survey 2008.

Figure 3.2 India's Public Reinsurance Program (the National Agricultural Insurance Scheme [NAIS])

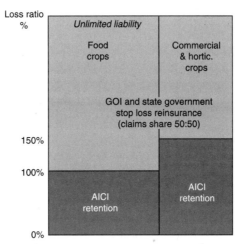

Source: AICI 2008.

agency, the Agricultural Insurance Company of India, Ltd. As such, it is not a conventional reinsurance program.

Portugal's System for the Protection of Climatic Risks (SIPAC) is a PPP for agricultural insurance and reinsurance. Under this program, the government provides voluntary crop stop-loss reinsurance protection to individual crop insurance companies according to defined agricultural risk zones (A–E) (figure 3.3). The program provides reinsurance protection for 85 percent of all losses in excess of a loss ratio of 65 percent in risk zone E, 80 percent in zone D, and 120 percent in zones A–C.

The Spanish combined agricultural insurance program is Europe's largest agricultural insurance program, covering crops, livestock, aquaculture, and forestry (figure 3.4). The program is underwritten by Agroseguro, a pool of 35 coinsurers. Consorcio Nacional de Compensacion de Seguros, Spain's national catastrophe reinsurer, provides comprehensive stop-loss reinsurance for Agroseguro. For viable lines, Consorcio offers layered stop-loss protection for losses in excess of a 78 percent loss ratio up to a 160 percent loss ratio, beyond which Consorcio assumes 100 percent of the losses. For experimental lines,

Figure 3.3 Portugal's Reinsurance Program (the System for the Protection of Climatic Risks [SIPAC])

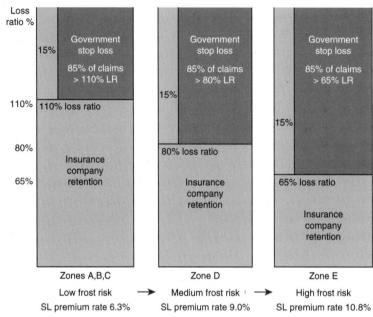

which include systemic perils of drought, flood, and livestock diseases, Consorcio provides excess-of-loss reinsurance. International reinsurers participate both in the viable lines' stop-loss program, where they reinsure the retentions of the pool coinsurers, and in a multiyear stop-loss retrocession cover for Consorcio.

The Mauritius Sugar Insurance Fund Board—a catastrophe windstorm and drought insurance scheme—has operated successfully since its formation in 1947 (figure 3.5). The program is reinsured under a layered stop-loss treaty program by a panel of international agricultural reinsurers. In 2007 the program reinsured losses in excess of a 95 percent loss ratio up to a 300 percent loss ratio in three layers.

In Mexico the parastatal agricultural reinsurance company, Agroasemex, provides reinsurance support to the private commercial agricultural insurance sector, to the mutual crop and livestock insurance schemes for

Figure 3.4 Spain's Reinsurance Program (Consorcio Reinsurance of Agroseguro)

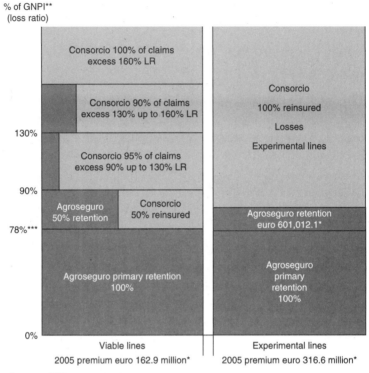

Source: Agroseguro 2007.
* Consorcio 2005, the Spanish model for catastrophe risk management, Istanbul 8–9/12/2005
** GNPI is equivalent to the commercial premium (prima commercial)
*** Pure risk premium with security margin (prima de riesgo regargado) is about 78% of commercial premium

small farmers (the Fondos program), and to state governments under the Fund for Agricultural Calamities (FAPRACC) program, which involves a series of new macro- or state-level parametric drought insurance schemes.

Reinsurance capacity is widely available for crop hail and named-peril crop insurance programs, which are not subject to catastrophe losses. In the World Bank survey, 73 percent of respondents identified no constraints to accessing their crop hail or named-peril capacity requirements (table 3.18). Nearly half of all respondents identified moderate to severe constraints in accessing reinsurance capacity for MPCI business. This finding is not surprising given the aversion of many international reinsurers to underwriting individual grower MPCI because of its exposure to systemic risks, which can result in catastrophic losses.

Figure 3.5 Mauritius Reinsurance Program (the Sugar Insurance Fund Private)

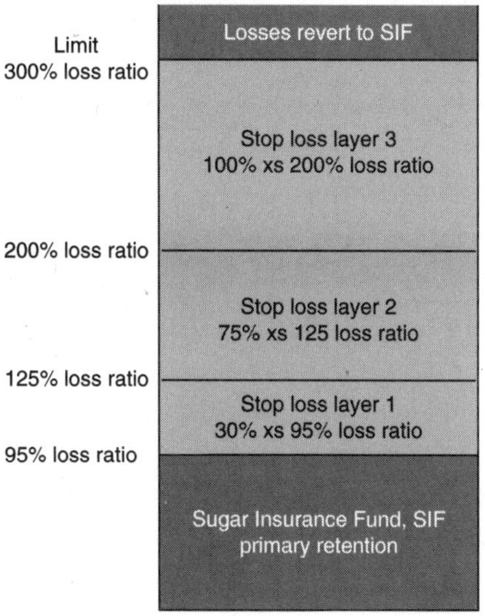

Source: Authors.

Table 3.18 Access to Agricultural Reinsurance Capacity for Different Product Lines (percent, except where otherwise indicated)

Class of agricultural insurance	Number of countries responding	No constraint	Moderate constraint	Major constraint
Crop hail/named peril	41	73	17	10
Multiple peril crop insurance	42	52	43	5
Livestock mortality	42	64	24	12
Livestock epidemic disease	31	39	23	39
Crop weather index	23	52	35	13
Other crop/livestock insurance	9	78	11	11
All	62	60	25	15

Source: World Bank Survey 2008.

Thirty-nine percent of respondents identified lack of access to reinsurance capacity for livestock epidemic disease cover as a major constraint. Lower-middle-income countries identifying this as a major constraint include China, Colombia, Mongolia, and Ukraine.

Lack of access to crop weather index reinsurance capacity is a moderate or severe constraint in nearly half of surveyed countries. This average number conceals a high level of heterogeneity. Countries like India, which underwrote about $412 million of total sum insured in 2008, do not face any constraints in placing their business on the reinsurance market (as long as the products are properly designed and rated). Countries involved in small pilots may not attract reinsurers, because of the small size of the business, although reinsurers have shown considerable interest in these new business opportunities, including small pilots.

Public Intervention in Agricultural Insurance

Public intervention in agricultural insurance is usually justified to correct market or regulatory imperfections. It can take various forms, the most common of which is direct premium subsidies. The fiscal cost of government-sponsored agricultural insurance programs can be high and even unsustainable for developing countries with limited fiscal space.

Types of Public Intervention

Governments often justify intervention in agricultural insurance on the following grounds:

- Insurance infrastructure of private crop and livestock insurance products and services are not available.

- Commercial insurers are reluctant to develop agricultural insurance programs because of the prohibitively high start-up costs.

- Private commercial insurers often face reinsurance capacity constraints to underwriting systemic risks.

- Insurers are deterred by the high administrative costs of underwriting crop and livestock insurance for small farmers.

- Small and marginal farmers cannot afford the often high costs of agricultural insurance premiums.

These issues are analyzed in detail in chapter 2. This section examines the most common forms of government intervention, as revealed by the survey.

The most common type of government intervention in crop insurance is premium subsidies, which 63 percent of surveyed countries provide. The incidence of subsidies is similar across regions, irrespective of economic status, except for the poorest low-income countries, only 40 percent of which provide crop premium subsidies (table 3.19).

Half of the surveyed countries have some form of crop insurance legislation, with marked differences across regions. In Europe 71 percent of countries have some forms of crop insurance legislation. The figure is just 30 percent in Latin America and the Caribbean.

Governments provide financial support to crop reinsurance in 32 percent of the surveyed countries. The incidence of reinsurance is especially high in Asia, where 70 percent of countries—including China, India, Iran, Japan, Kazakhstan, Korea, and Mongolia—report government support. There is a marked inverse relationship between the economic development status of a country and government support to reinsurance. No governments in low-income countries provide crop reinsurance; in high-income countries, 52 percent of countries surveyed support crop reinsurance programs, including the governments of Canada, the United States, and 38 percent of European countries. In Latin America and the Caribbean, which traditionally had a high level of government intervention in all classes of reinsurance (often in the form of monopoly public sector reinsurers), only two countries—Brazil and Mexico—report government support to crop reinsurance.

Governments subsidize the A&O costs of crop insurance in 16 percent of surveyed countries. This form of subsidization is particularly common in Asia (India, Japan, Korea, the Philippines). In 6 percent of countries, governments subsidize the costs of crop loss assessment. In India the government originally introduced seasonal crop cutting to establish national crop production and yield statistics rather than to measure crop yields for insurance purpose.

Australia and New Zealand are conspicuous for the absence of government financial intervention in agricultural crop and livestock insurance. In both countries, private commercial insurers actively compete for business with no subsidy distortions. The very large nonsubsidized crop hail insurance markets in Argentina and the United States also function without government intervention.

Table 3.19 Government Support to Crop Insurance, by Development Status and Region (percent, except where otherwise indicated)

Development status/region	Number of countries with crop insurance	Insurance legislation	Insurance premium subsidies	Administrative and operational subsidies	Loss assessment subsidies	Public sector reinsurance	Other support (R&D, training)
Development Status							
High-income	21	67	67	24	14	52	38
Upper-middle-income	18	50	56	6	0	22	39
Lower-middle-income	19	42	74	21	5	21	53
Low-income	5	20	40	0	0	0	60
Region							
Africa	8	38	63	0	0	13	38
Asia	10	60	70	40	20	70	70
Europe	21	71	67	10	5	38	29
Latin America and the Caribbean	20	30	60	10	0	5	45
North America	2	100	100	100	50	100	100
Oceania	2	0	0	0	0	0	50
All countries	63	51	63	16	6	32	44

Source: World Bank Survey 2008.

In 44 percent of surveyed countries, governments provide other forms of support. Such support includes funding of research and development (R&D) into new crop insurance products and programs and awareness education and training for farmers and agricultural insurance staff.

Government intervention is much less common in livestock insurance than crop insurance: only 35 percent of surveyed countries subsidize livestock premiums. The largest subsidized livestock insurance markets include China, Iran, Japan, Mexico, and Spain. The governments of Australia, France, and Germany, all of which have large livestock insurance sectors, provide no support. Livestock premium subsidies are available in three of the six low-income territories analyzed: Nepal (on a restricted basis), Nigeria, and Senegal. Public sector financial support to livestock reinsurance is provided in 26 percent of surveyed countries with livestock insurance (table 3.20).

Types of crop premium subsidies and premium subsidy levels. The type of crop insurance premium subsidy varies widely by region and to a lesser extent by development status (table 3.21).

The most common form of premium subsidy is a fixed (proportional) subsidy level for all insurable crops, types of farmers, and regions (35 percent of surveyed countries). This is followed by subsidies that vary according to crop types, farmer types, and other factors (27 percent of surveyed countries). In several countries with major crop insurance programs—including Argentina, Australia, Germany, South Africa, Sweden, and crop hail insurance in the United States—premiums are not subsidized.

One country, India, caps NAIS premium rates at 1.5–3.5 percent for food crops (that is, at about 33 percent of the estimated actuarial rates). The most common fixed premium subsidy level is 50 percent of the premium rate, irrespective of the crop or the actual premium rate, but in some countries the fixed rate is higher (80 percent in Italy, 70 percent in Guatemala) (see appendix D).

Some countries base crop premium subsidy levels on the type of insurance program, the coverage level, or the crop type and region. In Europe, Portugal and Spain use differential crop insurance premium subsidy levels to promote insurance for specific crops, types of farmers, and regions. They base their subsidies on criteria that include the type of crop (premiums on

Table 3.20 Government Support to Livestock Insurance, by Development Status and Region (percent, except where otherwise indicated)

Development status/region	Number of countries with livestock insurance	Insurance legislation	Insurance premium subsidies	Administrative and operational subsidies	Loss assessment subsidies	Public sector reinsurance	Other support (R&D, training)
Development Status							
High-income	19	53	42	26	16	32	42
Upper-middle-income	15	33	27	7	0	20	20
Lower-middle-income	14	14	29	0	7	36	43
Low-income	6	17	50	0	0	0	33
All countries	54	33	35	11	7	26	37
Region							
Africa	7	14	29	0	0	0	43
Asia	11	36	64	18	18	73	36
Europe	19	58	37	11	5	21	32
Latin America and the Caribbean	13	0	15	0	0	8	23
North America	2	100	50	100	50	50	100
Oceania	2	0	0	0	0	0	50
All countries	54	33	35	11	7	26	37

Source: World Bank Survey 2008.

Table 3.21 Type of Crop Insurance Premium Subsidy, by Development Status and Region (percent, except where otherwise indicated)

Development status/region	Number of countries with crop insurance	Type of crop premium subsidy				Special programs/ premium subsidies for small and marginal farmers
		Fixed	Variable	Capped premiums	No premium subsidies	
Development Status						
High-income	21	33	33	0	33	5
Upper-middle-income	18	28	28	0	44	11
Lower-middle-income	19	42	26	5	26	21
Low-income	5	40	0	0	60	20
Region						
Africa	8	63	0	0	38	0
Asia	10	30	40	10	20	10
Europe	21	48	19	0	33	5
Latin America and the Caribbean	20	20	35	0	45	25
North America	2	0	100	0	0	0
Oceania	2	0	0	0	100	0
All countries	63	35	27	2	35	11

Source: World Bank Survey 2008.

Box 3.5 Brazil's Crop-Credit Insurance Guarantee Program for Small and Marginal Farmers

The Brazilian Insurance for Family Agriculture (Seguro da Agricultura Familiar [SEAF]) is a compulsory crop credit insurance program for small-holder farmers who access seasonal production credit from the National Program for the Strengthening of Family Agriculture (Programa Nacional de Fortalecimento da Agricultura Familiar [PRONAF]). The features of this federal program include the following:

Nature of cover: Automatic cover for beneficiaries of PRONAF seasonal credit

Type of policy: Multiple peril yield shortfall policy, which indemnifies growers by the amount that actual crop revenue falls short of the sum insured

Insured crops: Wide range of crops identified under the agricultural zoning program (*zoneamento agricola*), including rainfed and irrigated cereals, legumes, oilseeds, fiber crops, root crops (cassava), grapes, and tree fruits

Insured perils: Drought, excess rain, frost, hail, excess variation in temperatures, strong winds, cold winds, crop pests, and diseases that are uncontrollable either technically or economically

Basis of sum insured: The sum insured is based on the amount of seasonal production credit loaned to the farmer plus the interest due on the principal plus up to 65 percent of the estimated net revenue of the crop, subject to a maximum of R$2,500 per farmer. The estimated gross and net revenue are determined by the bank and the crop inspector at the time of policy issuance.

Premium rate: 2 percent fixed rate, paid by the insured for each insured crop

Premium subsidy: The government pays a 75 percent premium subsidy on the SEAF program.

Basis of indemnity: Losses must exceed 30 percent of the expected gross revenue for the crop in order to qualify for an indemnity.

Source: Authors.

more susceptible crops are more heavily subsidized); the region (premiums in regions in which the government is promoting agriculture are more heavily subsidized); type of farmer (in France and Spain, young farmers can obtain an additional premium subsidy); the type of insurance contract (group contracts receive an additional subsidy); and the term of the contract (premiums on multiyear contracts are more heavily subsidized than annual contracts).

Several countries in Latin America and the Caribbean, including Brazil and Chile, cap the amount of premium subsidies a farmer can receive. This measure is designed to prevent large farmers from capturing a disproportionate percentage of the premium subsidy budget available each year. Other counties, such as Costa Rica, offer higher premium subsidy levels to small and marginal farmers than to larger farmers.

Special programs for small and marginal farmers. Several countries (11 percent of total) have developed special agricultural insurance delivery channels or programs for small and marginal farmers or provide special premium subsidy support to these farmers (see appendix D). In India, for example, small and marginal farmers qualify for premium subsidies of 10 percent of crop premiums on top of the capped premium rates. In Costa Rica small and marginal farmers qualify for 65 percent premium subsidy levels, medium-size farmers 55 percent premium subsidies, and large farmers 40 percent premium subsidies.

Other countries have developed specific programs for small farmers. In Brazil the federal government has two special crop insurance programs for small and marginal farmers (box 3.5). In Chile the National Development Agency (Instituto de Desarrollo Agropecuario [INDAP]) and the central bank, in conjunction with Magallanes Insurance Company, developed an online computerized crop insurance system that permits any recipient of seasonal crop production credit to be automatically instated under the small farmer insurance facility. In Mexico, Agroasemex has supported the Fondos crop and livestock mutual insurance funds for small farmers for nearly two decades. It provides technical support and training in underwriting and loss assessment as well as stop-loss reinsurance support for the Fondos. In Peru the government is supporting a program called Agro Proteje, which targets small and marginal farmers. In the Philippines, the mandate of the Philippines Crop Insurance Corporation is to focus on small farmers.

Quantifying the types of farmers who purchase crop and livestock insurance was outside the scope of this study; it is therefore not possible to determine whether the main beneficiaries of crop insurance are commercial or small and marginal farmers. Useful insights can, however, be drawn from India's NAIS, the world's largest crop insurance scheme in terms of number of farmers covered (in 2007 the program insured 18.4 million farmers, 16 percent of all farmers in India). NAIS is mandatory for farmers who access seasonal crop loans from the national and state-level agricultural banks and voluntary for nonborrowers. The scheme targets small and marginal farmers owning less than 2.5 hectares of land (about 80 percent of all farmers in India own less than 2 hectares of land). Small and marginal farmers accounted for two-thirds of all farmers insured under the scheme, but they received only one-third of the total value of claims settlements made by NAIS (because of the small size of their farms and insured cultivated area) (table 3.22). There are significant differences in the type of insured farmer by type of crop. Eighty percent of NAIS farmers insuring paddy (the staple food crop in India) were small and marginal farmers; they received 55 percent by value of all claims paid for paddy. Small and marginal farmers accounted for no more than half of insurance contracts for cash crops, including sunflower, bajra, red gram, soya bean, jowar, and horse gram.

Costs of Public Sector Agricultural Insurance Interventions

Agricultural insurance premium subsidies in the 65 surveyed countries cost governments $6.6 billion, or 44 percent of total global agricultural premiums, in 2007. Of this sum, $5.8 billion went toward subsidies of crop insurance premiums (47 percent of crop premiums in countries with crop premium subsidies) and $0.8 billion went toward subsidies of livestock insurance premiums (55 percent of livestock premiums in countries with livestock premium subsidies). About $5.3 billion of crop premium subsidies (91 percent of total crop premium subsidies) was distributed to farmers in 14 high-income countries, with $4.4 billion of total crop subsidies concentrated in Canada and the United States alone (table 3.23). The remaining $500 million of crop insurance premium subsidies was distributed among 24 upper-middle-income and lower-middle-income countries. Crop premium subsidies in low-income countries were minimal: only two countries—Nigeria and Senegal—provided subsidies at all. The program was not operational in Senegal in 2007, and the program in Nigeria was very small.

Table 3.22 Portion of Small and Marginal Farmers Benefiting from India's NAIS, 2000–07

Item	2000	2001	2002	2003	2004	2005	2006	2007	Average
Kharif Seasons									
Percentage of farmers covered	65	65	67	66	63	61	60	63	64
Percentage of total value claims	34	24	22	22	37	52	32	—	32
Rabi Seasons									
Percentage of farmers covered	71	71	75	69	55	66	62	60	65
Percentage of total value claims	44	41	40	49	29	64	49	—	42
Small and marginal farmers covered (percentage of all farmers covered)									65
Total value of claims for small and marginal farmers (percentage of total value of claims)									34

Source: James and Nair 2009.

Note: — = Not available.

Table 3.23 Estimated Cost of Crop Insurance Premium Subsidies, by Development Status and Region

Development status and region	Countries without crop insurance premium subsidies		Countries with crop insurance premium subsidies				All countries	Total crop premium subsidies ($ million)
	Number of countries	Crop premium ($ million)	Number of countries	Crop premium ($ million)	Premium subsidies ($ million)	Percent premium subsidy		
Development Status								
High-income	7	833.3	14	11,035.7	5,295.8	48	21	11,869.0
Upper-middle-income	8	277.5	10	595.1	272.6	46	18	872.6
Lower-middle-income	5	3.1	14	786.2	240.3	31	19	789.3
Low-income	3	0.2	2	0.0	—	0	5	0.2
Region								
Africa	3	21.2	5	37.3	3.9	11	8	58.5
Asia	3	5.6	7	1,260.3	468.8	37	10	1,265.9
Europe	7	308.1	14	1,794.6	869.1	48	21	2,102.6
Latin America and the Caribbean	8	245.9	12	215.4	98.0	46	20	461.3
North America[a]	1	487.8	2	9,109.3	4,368.9	48	2	9,597.2
Oceania	2	45.6	0	0	0	0	2	45.6
Total	23	1,114.1	40	12,416.9	5,808.7	47	63	13,531.1

Source: World Bank Survey 2008.

Note: — = Not available.

[a] The United States has both subsidized and nonsubsidized crop insurance programs.

For livestock, 74 percent of premium subsidies were concentrated in high-income countries. Asia was the most important region for livestock premium subsidies (table 3.24).

The top 10 government-subsidized agricultural insurance nations accounted for $13.4 billion (89 percent) of total agricultural insurance premiums in 2007 and $6.5 billion (98 percent) of total premium subsidies. The other 55 countries accounted for $1.7 billion of premium (11 percent of total agricultural insurance premium volume) and $135 million of premium subsidies (2 percent of total premium subsidies) (table 3.25).

The United States spent $3.8 billion in 2007 on crop premium subsidies, equivalent to 45 percent of total U.S. crop MPCI and hail premium volume or two-thirds of global crop premium subsidies. In contrast, livestock insurance is very limited in the United States, with 2007 premium subsidies amounting to just $165,000.

Spain ranked number 2 in 2007, with total premium subsidies of $580 million. Both crop and livestock insurance are very important. The 2007 average premium subsidy levels of 70 percent for crops and 74 percent for livestock were among the highest subsidy levels in Europe. Italy also provided very high average crop premium subsidies, of 74 percent.[8]

Japan is the third-largest country by premium subsidy volume and the most important livestock insurance market. It is closely followed by Canada, which is mainly a crop insurance market, with very limited livestock insurance.

There has been a major increase in crop and livestock premium subsidies in China since 2005. Under the 11th Five-Year Plan, China is investing heavily in agriculture. It is promoting agricultural insurance through a series of very ambitious national and regional projects for key food crops and livestock backed by central government and provincial government premium subsidies. The first agricultural insurance premium subsidies were not introduced in China until 2003. In 2005 total agricultural insurance premium in China was less than $100 million, and premium subsidies amounted to less than $40 million. In 2007 the Chinese government launched two major new subsidized insurance programs, including a national breeding sow epidemic disease program and a new MPCI program for six provinces. In 2007 agricultural insurance premiums

Table 3.24 Estimated Cost of Livestock Insurance Premium Subsidies, by Development Status and Region

Development status/region	Countries without livestock insurance premium subsidies		Countries with livestock insurance premium subsidies				All countries	Total livestock premium ($ million)
	Number of countries	Livestock premium ($ million)	Number of countries	Livestock premium ($ million)	Premium subsidies ($ million)	Percent premium subsidy		
Development Status								
High-income	10	149.3	9	1,043.1	556.1	53	19	1,192.3
Upper-middle-income	10	2.1	5	38.0	14.6	38	15	40.1
Lower-middle-income	12	1.1	2	333.0	215.4	65	14	334.1
Low-income	3	0.0	3	4.8	0.1	2	6	4.8
Region								
Africa	4	0.4	3	4.6	—	—	7	5.0
Asia	5	0.2	6	1,046.9	551.8	53	11	1,047.1
Europe	12	96.4	7	338.4	225.7	67	19	434.8
Latin America and the Caribbean	10	0.5	3	25.8	8.5	33	13	26.3
North America	1	0.0	1	3.2	0.2	5	2	3.2
Oceania	2	54.9	0	0.0	0.0	0	2	54.9
Total	34	152.4	20	1,418.9	786.2	55	54	1,571.4

Source: World Bank Survey 2008.
Note: — = Not available.

Table 3.25 Top 10 Providers of Agricultural Insurance Premium Subsidies, 2007 (millions of dollars, except where otherwise indicated)

Country	Crop insurance			Livestock insurance			Crop and livestock insurance		
	Premium	Premium subsidy	Premium subsidy as percentage of total premiums	Premium	Premium subsidy	Premium subsidy as percentage of total premiums	Premium	Premium subsidy	Premium subsidy as percentage of total premiums
United States[a]	8,508	3,823	45	3	0.2	5	8,511	3,823	45
Spain	514	362	70	295	220	74	809	581	72
Japan	446	229	51	665	319	48	1,111	549	49
Canada	1,090	546	50	0	0	N/A	1,090	546	50
Italy	381	280	73	2	0	0	383	280	73
China	423	132	31	259	151	58	682	283	41
Russian Federation	315	156	50	0	0	N/A	315	156	50
Iran, Islamic Rep. of	167	82	49	74	64	87	241	146	61
Mexico	123	53	43	20	8	40	142	62	43
Korea, Rep. of	59	17	29	34	17	50	93	34	37
Top 10 Countries	12,023	5,680	47	1,352	780	58	13,375	6,460	48
Other 55 Countries	1,508	128	8	219	6	3	1,727	135	8
Total	13,531	5,809	43	1,571	786	50	15,102	6,595	44

Source: World Bank Survey 2008.

a. Includes the subsidized FCIP, with estimated 2007 original gross premium of $8.02 billion, and unsubsidized crop hail premium of $490 million.

amounted to $682 million, and premium subsidies reached $283 million (41 percent of premiums) (see table 3.25). In 2008 the Chinese government increased its premium subsidies for crops from 50 percent to 60 percent (financed 35 percent by the central government and 25 percent by provincial governments). It increased the subsidy for the national breeding sow program from 60 percent to 80 percent (financed 50 percent by the central government and 30 percent by provincial governments) and the subsidy for the national breeding cow epidemic disease program from 40 percent to 60 percent. In 2008 the cost of agricultural insurance premiums in China was estimated at about $1.8 billion, with premium subsidies of about $1.1 billion, making China the second-largest agricultural insurance market in the world (Air Worldwide 2009).

In Brazil the federal government ratified the reintroduction of premium subsidies in 2005 and was projecting an increase of financial support for premium subsidies from $1 million in 2005 to $50 million in 2007 and to $100 million by 2009. Chile introduced premium subsides in 2001. France and Turkey introduced premium subsidies in 2005. Korea introduced crop premium and livestock premium subsidies in 2002; in 2007 it ranked 10th in the world in terms of premium subsidies.

In several countries, including Canada, India, Korea, and the United States, governments also subsidize A&O expenses of agricultural insurers (table 3.26). In the United States, the 17 insurance companies that underwrite the FCIP/multiple peril crop insurance program received $1.3 billion in 2007 to cover their marketing and acquisition costs and own administration and loss assessment costs. With the inclusion of other program fund costs, total A&O costs amounted to $1.5 billion (18.2 percent of estimated 2007 total original gross premiums). When this is added to the $3.8 billion of farmer premium subsidies, the total 2007 costs of subsidies amounts to $5.2 billion (66 percent of total premiums), a subsidy of $1.90 for every $1 in premiums paid by farmers. The A&O cost subsidies paid by the government in Canada are equivalent to 5.7 percent of total premiums; they amount to 27.5 percent of premiums in Korea and 3.0 percent of premiums in India's NAIS. The overall livestock A&O premium subsidies in the surveyed countries amounted to a much more modest $6.0 million in 2007.

Table 3.26 Estimated Costs of Administration and Operating Expense Subsidies, 2007

Country	2007 total original gross premium ($ million)	Crop premium subsidies ($ million)	A&O expense subsidies ($ million)	Total subsidies on premiums ($ million)	Average government settled claims ($ million)[a]	Total subsidy percentage
Crop Insurance						
Canada	1,089.5	545.7	62.5	608.2	—	56
India	149.8	7.9	4.4	12.3	241.3	169
Japan	445.8	229.3	—	229.3	95.4	73
Korea, Rep. of	58.7	17.0	16.1	33.2	—	57
United States (FCIP only)[b]	8,019.8	3,823.1	1,458.0	5,281.1	1,569.4	85
All surveyed countries	13,531.1	5,809.0	1,540.9	7,349.9	1,906.1	68
Livestock						
Japan	665.2	319.3	0.0	319.3	198.3	78
Korea, Rep. of	34.3	17.0	5.3	22.3	0.0	65
Mongolia	0.1	0.0	0.0	0.0	0.1	136
United States	3.2	0.2	—	0.2	0.0	5
All surveyed countries	1,571.4	786.2	6.0	792.8	198.4	63

Source: World Bank Survey 2008.

Note: — = Not available.

a. For countries other than the United States, this number is the average government settled claims in 2003–07 or total number of years for which data were available.

b. FCIP total crop original gross premium was $6.56 billion net premium plus $1.45 billion total A&O expenses. In addition, in 2007 a total net underwriting outlay of $1.57 billion was paid to insurers under the Standard Reinsurance Agreement.

Governments in several countries, including India, Japan, Mongolia, and the United States, paid excess claims (reinsured). In the United States, the government reinsures the FCIP both on a proportional and nonproportional basis under the Special Reinsurance Agreement; in 2007 the government's net underwriting outlay amounted to $1.6 billion.

The total public cost of agricultural insurance programs is estimated at 68 percent of the 2007 global premium volume, of which upfront premium subsidies represent 44 percent. Including A&O subsidies and claim subsidies, the total cost to government of agricultural insurance provision may be as high as 68 percent of original gross premiums. Continuance of these trends over the next few years would place a major financial burden on national governments, particularly in low- and middle-income countries, few of which can afford to fund public subsidy programs as generous as those in the high-income countries covered by this survey.

Government subsidies of agricultural insurance range greatly (figure 3.6). India has the highest percentage levels of government subsidy support as a percentage of original gross premiums. It provides very low upfront premium subsidy support, given the design of the NAIS, but once the costs of settling excess claims are included, total subsidies amount to 169 percent of 2007 original gross premiums.

As a percentage of producer premiums, the highest subsidy levels are in Europe, where the average 2007 premium subsidy levels were 74 percent in Italy, 72 percent in Spain, and 67 percent in Portugal (figure 3.6b). In Italy and Spain, the cost of premium subsidies in 2007 exceeded 275 percent of the premiums paid by insured farmers (that is, for every $1 of premium collected from farmers, premium subsidies exceeded $2.75). The European Union has taken advantage of World Trade Organization legislation to increase agricultural insurance premium subsidy levels to a maximum of 80 percent of premium.

In the United States, total subsidies on FCIP crop and livestock premiums and A&O expenses (plus reinsurance subsidies through the standard reinsurance agreement) amounted to 85 percent of total original gross premiums in 2007—a cost of $2.50 in federal subsidies for every $1 of premium paid by farmers. In 2007 the Chinese national and provincial governments embarked on a major program of subsidized crop and livestock insurance and premium subsidies that cost $283 million, or 41 percent of total agricultural crop and livestock premiums. For 2008 the

Figure 3.6 Estimated Cost of Government Subsidies in Selected Countries, 2007

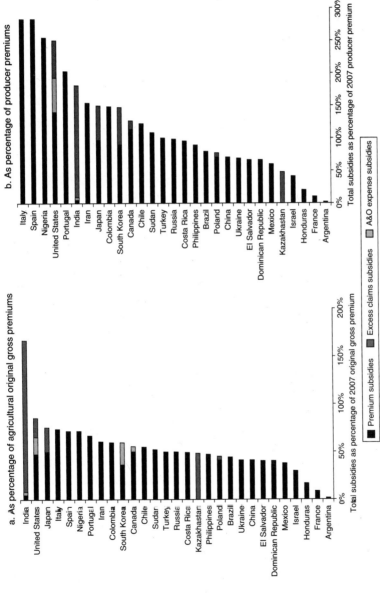

a. As percentage of agricultural original gross premiums

Total subsidies as percentage of 2007 original gross premium

b. As percentage of producer premiums

Total subsidies as percentage of 2007 producer premium

■ Premium subsidies　■ Excess claims subsidies　▨ A&O expense subsidies

Source: World Bank Survey 2008.

Note: Kazakhstan's excess claims subsidies are based on the three-year average for 2004–07. The analysis for the United States is based only on the FCIP's subsidized MPCI and livestock programs (that is, it excludes private crop hail insurance).

117

Chinese government authorized an increase in maximum premium subsidy levels to 60 percent of total premium.

At the other end of the scale, government subsidies accounted for a very small proportion of premiums in Argentina, France, and Honduras. Argentina has implemented private commercial crop hail insurance for more than 100 years without any form of government intervention, but in recent years some provincial governments introduced subsidized crop insurance for specialist crops, including wine grapes and tree fruit.

Penetration of Agricultural Insurance

Not surprisingly, the highest agricultural insurance penetration rates are found in the group of high-income countries; within these countries, the highest penetration rates are in countries with very high levels of government premium subsidy support (figure 3.7 and table 3.27).[9] In the United States, the 2007 penetration rate for agricultural insurance was 5.2 percent of agricultural GDP (AGDP)—a higher penetrate rate than the 4.8 percent rate for non–life insurance.[10] It is followed by four other high-income countries with major public intervention in agricultural insurance: Canada (4.1 percent), Japan (1.8 percent), and Spain (1.6 percent).

In upper-middle-income and lower-middle-income countries, the highest agricultural insurance penetration rates are found in Argentina and Mauritius. In Argentina agricultural production accounted for more than 9 percent of GDP in 2007; the agricultural insurance penetration rate was 0.99 percent of agricultural gross domestic product. In Mauritius sugarcane accounts for nearly 90 percent of total cropped area and about 70 percent of the value of all agricultural production: under the Sugar Insurance Fund scheme, crop insurance is mandatory for all farmers, explaining the very high agricultural insurance penetration rate of 3.3 percent of agricultural gross domestic product (a rate that is far higher than the 1.6 percent penetration rate for non–life insurance). The next-highest agricultural insurance penetration rates are found in countries with major premium subsidy support, including Iran (0.8 percent penetration rate), Russia (0.6 percent rate), Bulgaria (0.5 percent rate),[11] and Mexico (0.4 percent rate).

Figure 3.7 Estimated Agricultural and Non–Life Insurance Penetration

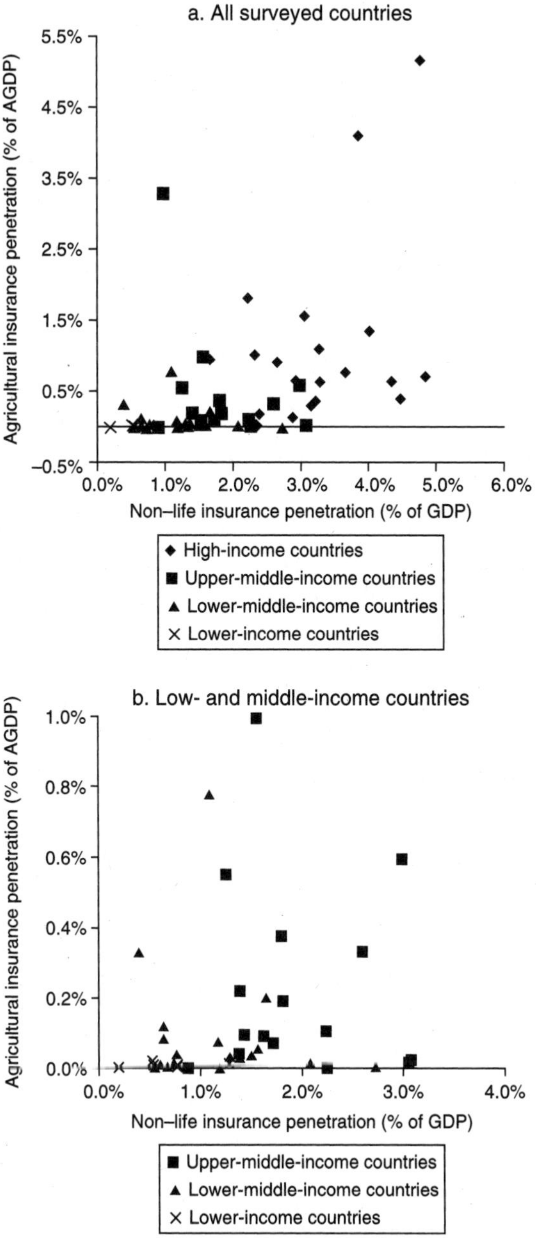
a. All surveyed countries
Agricultural insurance penetration (% of AGDP)
5.5%
4.5%
3.5%
2.5%
1.5%
0.5%
–0.5%
0.0%
1.0%
2.0%
3.0%
4.0%
5.0%
6.0%
Non–life insurance penetration (% of GDP)
High-income countries
Upper-middle-income countries
Lower-middle-income countries
Lower-income countries
b. Low- and middle-income countries
Agricultural insurance penetration (% of AGDP)
1.0%
0.8%
0.6%
0.4%
0.2%
0.0%
0.0%
1.0%
2.0%
3.0%
4.0%
Non–life insurance penetration (% of GDP)
Upper-middle-income countries
Lower-middle-income countries
Lower-income countries

Source: World Bank Survey 2008.

Table 3.27 Estimated Penetration Rates of Crop Insurance, by Development Status and Region, 2007

Development status/region	Percentage of farmers insured	Percentage of national area insured
Countries without Premium Subsidies		
High-income	41.7	39.1
Upper-middle-income	44.0	27.3
Lower-middle-income	8.0	2.0
Low-income	0.5	4.7
Countries with Premium Subsidies		
High-income	88.0	47.6
Upper-middle-income	26.7	26.8
Lower-middle-income	15.4	9.7

Source: World Bank Survey 2008.

Several major agricultural economies, including Brazil, China, and India, that had very high levels of public sector premium subsidy support in 2007 had low agricultural insurance penetration rates (0.11 percent of agricultural gross domestic product in Brazil, 0.20 percent in China, and 0.07 percent in India); there is considerable potential for expansion of agricultural insurance provision in these countries. In this context, although the agricultural insurance initiatives in Brazil and China are very new and have received government premium subsidy support only in recent years, penetration rates in both countries doubled between 2005 and 2008. The figures for India underestimate the true levels of agricultural insurance penetration, because under the NAIS scheme premium rates for food crops are capped at about 30 percent of the actuarial rates. Agricultural insurance penetration rates are extremely low in low-income countries. In no low-income country does penetration exceed 0.02 percent of agricultural gross domestic product.

Among countries with no government intervention or premium subsidy support in 2007, high crop insurance penetration rates for voluntary private sector crop hail and named-peril insurance are found in Switzerland (75 percent area insured), Sweden (52 percent), Australia (50 percent), and Argentina (48 percent). In Uruguay, another country with an unsubsidized crop hail market, about 68 percent of cultivated area was insured in 2007.[12] In the Windward Islands, the very high penetration rate of 62 percent for nonsubsidized banana windstorm insurance is explained by the fact that insurance is mandatory for all farmers (except in St. Lucia, where the Banana Insurance Act was never ratified).

For nonsubsidized private commercial insurance in most lower-middle-income and low-income countries, levels of penetration of crop insurance are very low. Most programs are at a pilot development stage (an exception is Ecuador, where crop insurance has been implemented for a decade).

In countries with premium subsidies, crop insurance penetration rates for voluntary and mature schemes are very high in Israel (90 percent of cropped area insured), the United States (90 percent), Canada (63 percent), Iran (35 percent), Spain (26 percent), and Mexico (21 percent).[13] In emerging economies, where subsidized agricultural crop insurance is relatively new, insurance uptake is high in Kazakhstan (61 percent of area insured), Russia (28 percent), Korea (26 percent),[14] and Sudan (10 percent).

Very few countries provided quantifiable data on the numbers of insured animals. The findings presented in appendix D are therefore only illustrative. In Germany, Hungary, and Sweden, which have competitive and well-developed nonsubsidized livestock insurance markets, voluntary livestock insurance uptake rates were very high in 2007 (50–70 percent of the national herd). Among countries in which livestock insurance is subsidized, Israel reported penetration rates of nearly 100 percent for cattle. India, Iran, Korea, Mexico, and Spain also report high levels of livestock insurance coverage.

Spain provides an interesting example of insurance penetration rates in a voluntary, mature agricultural insurance market that attracts very high levels of public sector premium subsidy and reinsurance support under a national PPP. The program has operated for 29 years throughout the country and is well known by Spanish crop and livestock producers. For high-value specialist crops, such as tobacco and bananas insurance penetration rates are on the order of 100 percent; in the case of citrus, tree fruit, and winter cereals, more than 50 percent of cultivated area is insured. For other crops, such as wine grapes and olives, less than 10 percent of cultivated area is insured. Overall, 26 percent of the national cultivated area was insured in 2007. For livestock, voluntary insurance uptake is less than 20 percent of the national herd, but in the case of compulsory carcass destruction cover, more than 220 million head of livestock and poultry (more than 95 percent of the national herd/flock) were insured in 2007.

The United States' FCIP/MPCI program has one of the highest uptake rates in the world. In 2007 the scheme insured 271 million acres (110 million hectares), or about 85 percent of all eligible crop acreage in the United States. MPCI penetration rates for major cereals rose from about 65 percent in 1998 to nearly 80 percent in 2006 (figure 3.8). This increase in insurance demand and penetration rates is attributed to increases in premium subsidy levels, increases in insured yield coverage levels and the expansion of crop revenue protection plans, the withdrawal of eligibility for government disaster relief payments for farmers who do not purchase a minimum level of FCIP crop insurance,[15] and major increases in crop commodity prices in recent years.

In conclusion, high levels of crop and livestock insurance uptake are found with programs that carry high premium subsidy levels, but named-peril crop insurance and livestock insurance penetration rates are equally high in countries with a strong tradition of agricultural insurance. There-fore, this survey does not support the argument that premium subsidies

Figure 3.8 Penetration Rates for Multiple Peril Crop Insurance in the United States, by Crop (percentage of eligible acres insured)

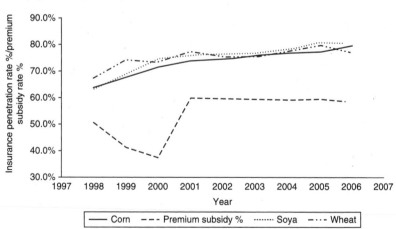

Source: Authors' analysis of U.S. Risk Management Agency MPCI data.

are necessary if farmers and livestock breeders are to purchase voluntary crop and livestock insurance.

Performance of Agricultural Insurance Providers

The financial performance of selected public and private sector agricultural insurance programs is analyzed below, using the financial data collected by the survey. Additional information is included in the individual country reports in appendix E.

Costs of Providing Agricultural Insurance

Many public sector agricultural insurance schemes were criticized in the 1980s for their high A&O costs (see, for example, Hazell 1992). Since then, the agricultural insurance market has changed dramatically, with increasing involvement of the private sector through PPP arrangements.

A&O expenses can be divided into three categories: marketing and acquisition costs (including commissions paid to agents and brokers); insurers' own administration expenses; and, where appropriate, the expense load added to cover loss adjustment expenses. These costs are expressed as a percentage of original gross premiums for 29 surveyed countries (figure 3.9).[16] Some companies do not estimate their loss adjustment expenses as a percentage of premium for premium gross-up purposes or could not provide details of their loss adjustment expenses. In some countries the costs are general agricultural insurance market estimates; in other countries companies were very transparent in providing their own cost structure information.

For the 29 sampled countries, the average cost structure was about 25–30 percent of original gross premiums. It is typically divided into 10–15 percent for marketing and acquisition costs, 5–10 percent for the company's own A&O expenses, and 3–5 percent for loss adjustment expenses. Cost structures in many private commercial crop hail markets are somewhat lower (23 percent in Australia, 22 percent in New Zealand, and 21 percent in South Africa, for example) than in subsidized MPCI programs in countries such as Brazil (36 percent), Mexico (30 percent), India (30 percent),[17] and the United States (26 percent). However, in Argentina, which is a hail market, costs average 30 percent. In Canada,

Figure 3.9 Costs of Providing Crop Insurance as Percentage of Original Gross Premiums in Selected Countries

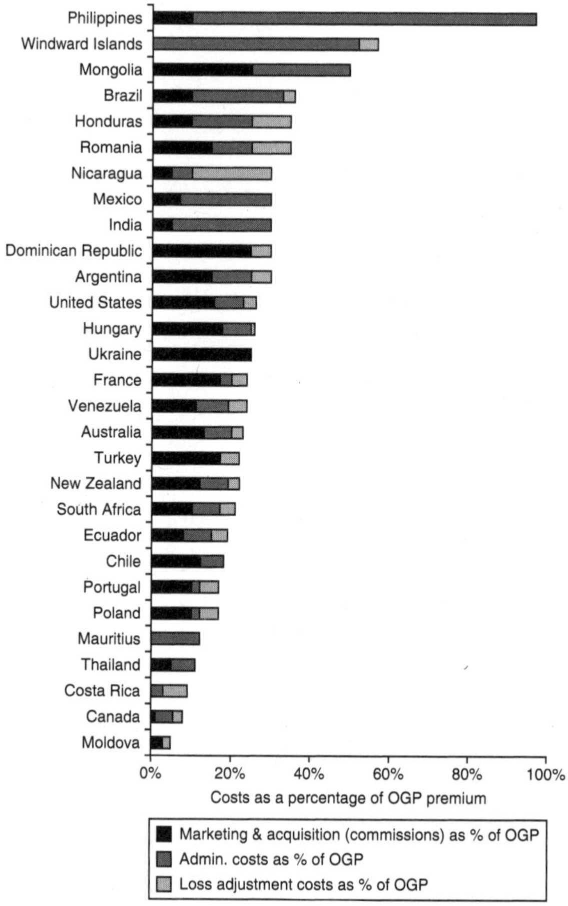

Costs as a percentage of OGP premium

- ■ Marketing & acquisition (commissions) as % of OGP
- ■ Admin. costs as % of OGP
- □ Loss adjustment costs as % of OGP

Source: World Bank Survey 2008.

which is a predominantly subsidized MPCI market, reported total costs are only 8 percent of original gross premiums (it is not clear if this figure underreports marketing and acquisition costs). The very high cost structures in the Philippines and Windward Islands are a function of major declines in the demand for crop and livestock insurance: in 2007 programs were operating on a commercial basis with technically calculated premium rates; underwriting results especially in the Philippines are profitable before A&O expenses are considered.

The average expenses of about 25 percent for crop insurance are not excessive. They conform to the ceding commission levels reinsurers are usually prepared to grant on quota share treaty business.

Profitability of Agricultural Insurance

The profitability of the agricultural insurance programs—in terms of five-year average loss ratios (the ratio of total gross claims to total original gross premiums) for 2003–07—is analyzed for selected countries (annual country data are presented in appendix E; the results are summarized in appendix D).[18] The results are presented separately for countries with and without crop and livestock premium subsidies (figure 3.10). The analysis is based on original gross premiums and claims; it does not include reinsurance arrangements.

Three subsidized programs—in India, Iran, and Poland—have five-year loss ratios that exceed 100 percent. India's NAIS program has a long-term average loss ratio exceeding 300 percent. NAIS premium rates are capped at 1.5–3.0 percent for food crops—well below the actuarially fair premium rate (estimated at 10 percent). State and central governments pay all claims that exceed the premium volume on a 50:50 basis. As a consequence of this program design, the average loss ratio of the NAIS well exceeds 100 percent. The Indian government has considered moving the NAIS to an actuarial regime. The Agricultural Insurance Company of India (AICI) would charge premiums on a commercial basis; where necessary, governmental support would provide upfront premium subsidies (though not for commercial/horticultural crops), differentiated by the economic category of farmer. AICI would receive "upfront" premium subsidies and handle all claims. These changes would help address the issue of delayed indemnity payments to farmers, because the government contribution, which currently leads to considerable delays in settlements, would be made upfront. Such a sound financial and actuarial approach would also introduce more discipline into the Indian crop insurance program and improve the targeting of subsidies for poorer farmers.

With average A&O expenses on the order of 25–30 percent of original gross premiums, any program incurring an average loss ratio higher than 70–75 percent incurs a combined ratio of more than 100 percent (that is,

Figure 3.10 Estimated Average Crop Loss Ratios in Selected Countries, 2003–07

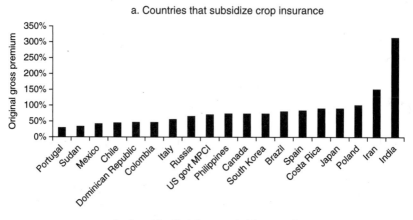

a. Countries that subsidize crop insurance

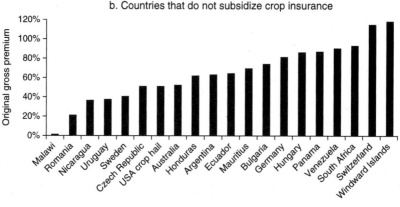

b. Countries that do not subsidize crop insurance

Source: World Bank Survey 2008.
Note: See appendix D for details.

it will not be charging adequate premiums to cover actual claims plus A&O expenses). This is the case for 8 of the 18 countries with crop premium subsidies (Brazil, India, Iran, Korea, Japan, the Philippines,[19] Poland, and Spain). The U.S. FCIP ran at a 70 percent loss ratio over the 2003–07 period.

Among private crop insurance programs carrying no premium subsidies, those in Switzerland and the Windward Islands incurred loss ratios greater than 100 percent over the 2003–07 period.[20] Other countries in which programs are unlikely to be profitable once total A&O expenses are accounted for include Germany (81 percent loss ratio), Hungary (86 percent loss ratio), Panama (87 percent loss ratio), República Bolivariana de Venezuela (90 percent crop loss ratio), and South Africa (93 percent loss ratio).

In the United States, the highly subsidized FCIP operated at an original loss ratio of 70 percent over the 2003–07 period (92 percent loss ratio over the 28-year period 1981–2008). In contrast, the private crop hail program in the United States, which is not subsidized, operated at a profitable loss ratio of 51 percent for 2003–07 and 67 percent for 1915–2005.

For livestock insurance, most unsubsidized programs are operating with average loss ratios of less than 60 percent, indicating they are operating profitably (figure 3.11). In contrast, only a few subsidized livestock insurance programs are operating at loss ratios of less than 70 percent.[21] With average expense ratios estimated at 30 percent for livestock insurance, countries whose loss ratios exceeded 70 percent incurred negative underwriting results over period.

Combining average loss ratios for crop and livestock insurance allows a broader range of countries to be compared (figure 3.12). Among countries that subsidize premiums, India, Iran, and Poland incurred overall loss ratios of 100 percent or more. Among countries that do not provide premium subsidies, overall loss ratios exceeded 100 percent in Mongolia, Switzerland, and the Windward Islands.

Producer Loss Ratios of Subsidized Crop and Livestock Programs

This section presents a reworked analysis of the five-year results (2003–07) for crop and livestock insurance programs that receive government premium subsidy support by calculating the loss ratio based on the (non-subsidized) portion of the premium paid by the farmer, or the "producer premium." The resulting net of premium subsidies loss ratio is termed the *producer loss ratio*. A producer loss ratio greater than 100 percent means the program is not collecting adequate premiums from producers to cover indemnity payments.

Very few subsidized crop or livestock insurance programs achieved producer loss ratios of less than 100 percent (exceptions include the

Figure 3.11 Estimated Average Livestock Loss Ratio in Selected Countries, 2003–07

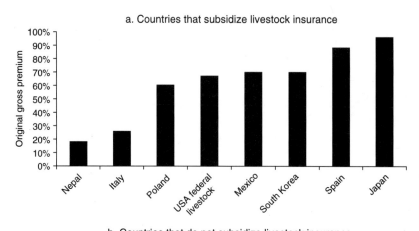

a. Countries that subsidize livestock insurance

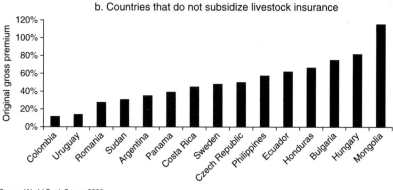

b. Countries that do not subsidize livestock insurance

Source: World Bank Survey 2008.
Note: See appendix D for details. The results for Mongolia should be interpreted with caution, as the program is a pilot catastrophe livestock mortality index cover that operated for just two of the five years in the study period and incurred very high losses in 2007.

Dominican Republic, Sudan, Mexico, Portugal, Chile, China, and Nepal) (figure 3.13). At the other extreme, in Iran, the heavily subsidized national crop and livestock insurance programs incurred a combined average producer loss ratio of 405 percent. In Europe, Spain and Italy have the largest subsidized crop and livestock insurance programs, with five-year average premium subsidy levels of 71 percent for crop insurance and 61 percent for livestock insurance. The producer loss was 294 percent in Spain and 147 percent in Italy. In the United States,

Figure 3.12 Estimated Average Crop and Livestock Loss Ratios in Selected Countries, 2003–07

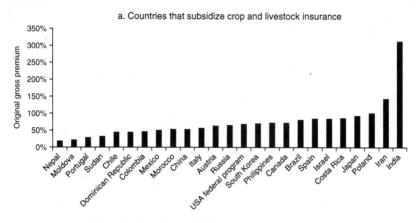

a. Countries that subsidize crop and livestock insurance

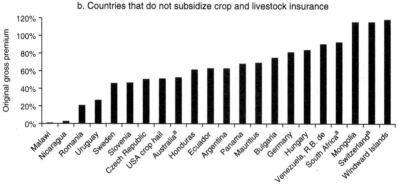

b. Countries that do not subsidize crop and livestock insurance

Source: World Bank Survey 2008.

Note: See appendix D for details.

[a] Country subsidizes livestock insurance, but survey data were insufficient to analyze livestock results. Only the crop insurance loss ratio is therefore presented.

the FCIP incurred an average producer loss ratio of 170 percent; the corresponding crop producer loss ratio was even higher in Canada, at 186 percent. (Once A&O and crop insurance delivery subsidies are taken into account in the United States and Canada, the costs to government are even higher.) In Asia, China is the only major crop and livestock insurer to show a producer loss ratio of less than 100 percent, but this result is biased by the fact that premium subsidies were introduced on a national scale only in 2007.

Figure 3.13 Estimated Average Producer Loss Ratio in Selected Countries, 2003–07

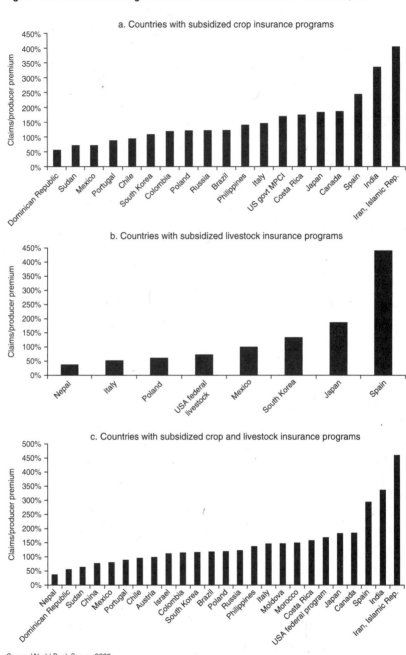

Source: World Bank Survey 2008.
Note: See appendix D for full results.

Comparative Performance of Public and Private Providers of Agricultural Insurance

Since Hazell (1992) produced his evaluation of the failure of public sector MPCI in the 1980s, there have been major developments in the field of agricultural insurance. Foremost among them has been the switch to mainly private sector–implemented agricultural insurance (stand-alone private sector schemes or schemes backed by government subsidies and other support under various forms of PPP). The survey results allow the performance of various types of programs to be compared.

In Brazil all public sector insurers had been replaced by private commercial insurance companies by 2007. The producer loss ratio was 123 percent for crops (119 percent for crops and livestock), down from 429 percent under the public sector Proagro in the 1980s (table 3.28). The market results for Brazil are biased toward the heavy losses incurred by COSESP, the former São Paulo state crop and insurer, which was terminated in 2005 following very poor underwriting results. The Brazilian market is, however, still very exposed to losses of the individual grower MPCI business.

In Mexico the former public sector insurer Anagsa was liquidated in 1990 and replaced by Agroasemex; the market was then opened up to private commercial insurance companies. The average underwriting results for 2003–07 show considerable improvement, with a producer loss ratio of 73 percent for crops or (80 percent for crops and livestock), down from 429 percent during the Anagsa period.

In India the government made a policy decision to continue to offer the NAIS at highly subsidized and low rates in order to meet its social responsibility of making seasonal crop credit linked to crop insurance widely available to small and marginal farmers. The 2000–08 average producer loss ratio of 336 percent represents an improvement over the 1980s, when this ratio was as high as 511 percent, but NAIS continues to operate at a financial loss. The government is considering moving to an actuarial regime for NAIS, in which premium rates would be charged on an actuarial basis and premium subsidies would be provided upfront.

In the Philippines, the Philippines Crop Insurance Corporation (PCIC) has significantly improved its underwriting results. It continues to face

Table 3.28 Estimated Financial Performance of Selected Agricultural Insurance Programs (percent, except where otherwise indicated)

Country/program	Period	Loss ratio	Producer loss ratio	Average premium rate charged to farmers
Public Sector Agricultural Insurance				
Canada (crop)	2003–07	74	186	10.3
Costa Rica (INS crop)	2003–07	90	176	6.3
India (NAIS)	2000–08	314	336	1.5–3.0
Philippines (PCIC)	2003–07	73	142	11.6 for crop insurance, 4.5 for livestock insurance
Private–Public Partnerships (government premium subsidies)				
Brazil (crop and livestock)[a]	2004–07	81	123	4.8 for crop insurance
Chile	2003–07	45	95	3.5–7.5
Japan (crop and livestock)	2003–08	94	184	3.5–5.0
Korea, Rep. of (crop and livestock)	2003–08	72	116	7.8 for crop insurance, 7.1 for livestock insurance
Mexico (crop and livestock)	2003–07	50	80	7.7 crop insurance, 1.6 for livestock insurance
Portugal (crop)	2003–07	29	88	6.7 (2–25)
Spain (crop and livestock)	2003–07	85	294	5.7 for crop insurance, 4.8 for livestock insurance
Sudan (crop and livestock)	2003–07	34	64	7.2 for crop insurance, 10.3 l for livestock insurance
United States (FCIP)	2003–07	70	170	8.0–10.0
Private Commercial Sector (no public premium subsidies)				
Argentina (crop)	2003–07	63	64	3.5–5.0
Australia (crop)	2003–07	52	52	3.5–7.5
Germany (crop)	2003–05	81	81	1.0–2.0 crop (for crop hail insurance)
South Africa (crop)	2004–07	93	93	3.0–5.0
Sweden (crop)	2003–07	40	40	3.0–5.0
United States (crop hail)	2004–07	51	51	2.80
Windward Islands (crop)	2003–07	118	118	10.0–20.0

Source: World Bank Survey 2008.
[a] Includes COSESP, public sector insurer until 2005–06.

very high A&O expenses. The subsidized PPP program in Japan shows producer loss ratios of 294 percent, because of the very high premium subsidies.

The FCIP program in the United States is rated to operate at a breakeven loss ratio (calculated on total premiums), but it represents a huge cost to the U.S. taxpayer, with a producer loss ratio of 170 percent over 2003–08, only slightly below the average of 187 percent when Hazell reviewed the program's performance in the 1990s. However, once delivery costs (A&O expense subsidies and reinsurance claims subsidies paid by government under the standard reinsurance agreement) are taken into account, the program cost the government an average of $3.89 per $1 of producer premium over the 2003–08 period and $2.08 per $1 of producer premium over the 1981–2008 period (see appendix D).

The subsidized PPP program in Spain shows producer loss ratios of 150 percent, because of the very high premium subsidies. The specialist agricultural insurer in Portugal had a producer loss ratio of 88 percent over the period (a period of frost-free years with no catastrophic losses).

Sudan has underwritten subsidized crop and livestock insurance for nearly a decade. Over the five-year period studied, its subsidized program generated underwriting profits, with an average producer loss ratio of 64 percent.

Results varied for private crop insurance markets. Underwriting results were negative in the Windward Islands, and loss ratios were high in Germany and South Africa. Underwriters in Argentina earned small profits (average total commission levels represented about 30 percent of original gross premiums). Profits were sustainable in Australia, Chile, Sweden, and especially the United States, where the private crop hail insurance industry is highly profitable to underwriters.

Notes

1. As with any questionnaire survey, data and information are not always recorded for each field. In some cases, errors may have been introduced in data entry and not detected by the authors. In order to compare financial figures across a wide number of territories, all original currency data were converted into U.S. dollars using average currency exchange rates for each year.

2. Developing countries that have or are developing some form of agricultural insurance but on which information could not be obtained include Cuba, Indonesia, Kenya, the Democratic People's Republic of Korea, Pakistan, Sri Lanka, Zambia, and Zimbabwe.

3. Hazell's ratios provide a measure of the full economic cost to government of subsidized agricultural insurance. They are distinct from ratios that do not distinguish between the proportion of original gross premium paid by the farmer and by the government. They do not measure the performance of the insurance company as a financially viable or nonviable entity. Rather, they are indicative of the cost of agricultural insurance relative to the cost borne by producers. Where the government subsidizes agricultural insurance heavily, Hazell's ratios are bound to be high.

4. The government of India has proposed moving the NAIS to an actuarial regime since 2006. Major changes would include the provision of upfront premium subsidies and the reinsurance of the NAIS on the private reinsurance market.

5. The authors estimate 2007 global agricultural insurance premiums at about $17.5 billion.

6. In some countries, large commercial farms that can demonstrate high levels of animal husbandry and control over animal diseases can purchase policies that include diseases. Such covers are normally offered for high-value bloodstock or herds.

7. Swiss Re and Paris Re are leaders in crop weather index reinsurance.

8. The reason for the very high premium subsidy levels in Spain and Italy is that European Union Common Agriculture Policy legislation currently permits premium subsidies to be a maximum of 80 percent of full premium for damage to crops and livestock caused by natural and climatic disasters and where damage exceeds 30 percent of the value of the insured good.

9. There is a high level of heterogeneity among surveyed countries even by development status. Therefore, the estimated penetration rates by development status should be viewed as illustrative. Appendix D presents subsidy rates for selected countries. Livestock data were not rich enough to permit estimation of livestock insurance penetration by country developmental status.

10. Of the 95 countries surveyed, the United States ranks second in the world after Switzerland in terms of the 2007 nonlife insurance penetration rate (nonlife premiums divided by GDP) (Cummins and Mahul 2009).

11. This figure is particularly high given that Bulgaria does not subsidize premiums.

12. Uruguay provides very restricted crop premium subsidies for fruit and horticultural crops. In 2007 these subsidies represented less than 1.5 percent of agricultural insurance premiums.

13. The 100 percent penetration in Mauritius applies only to sugarcane, which is insured on a compulsory basis.

14. This statistic applies only to the insured fruit sector.

15. The minimum level coverage is catastrophe cover, for which farmers currently pay a $300 administrative fee per crop per county, for coverage of 50 percent of their long-term average yield.

16. Start-up costs are not included in these costs. They can be significant, particularly when a new market is created or innovative index-based insurance products are developed. These costs are usually partially, if not totally, covered by the donors through international technical assistance.

17. The costs for the NAIS scheme in India are based on the authors' own estimates of the full A&O and delivery costs of the scheme.

18. A five-year period may be too short to capture the financial viability of a program, particularly when it is exposed to catastrophic losses. Within the scope of this survey, it was not deemed possible to collect more than five years of financial results from the respondents in each country.

19. The five-year average loss ratio in the Philippines is 73 percent. Because of the program's small size and high fixed A&O costs of 97 percent of original gross premiums, the combined ratio is a very high 170 percent.

20. The very high loss ratio in the Windward Islands is explained by the fact that the islands were badly hit by hurricanes in 2004 and 2006.

21. The analysis excludes Iran, whose highly subsidized livestock insurance program incurred loses of 624 percent over the 2003–07 period.

Options for and Challenges to Providing Public Support to Agricultural Insurance in Developing Countries

T his chapter presents some conclusions on and recommendations for the development of sustainable agricultural insurance programs. It is based on the rationale for public intervention in agricultural insurance presented in chapter 2, the review of 65 national agricultural insurance schemes presented in chapter 3, and World Bank experience with agricultural insurance over the past decade. The conclusions and recommendations are intended to provide a policy framework with which governments, particularly in developing countries, can promote and enhance sustainable and cost-effective, market-based agricultural insurance.

The chapter also addresses key challenges—institutional, financial, technical, and operational—governments face in developing agricultural insurance markets. The importance of these challenges is likely to differ from country to country, depending on the level of development of the agricultural sector, the degree of maturity of domestic insurance markets, and the level of modernization of the agricultural sector.

Agricultural insurance has major limitations. It is a low priority for many poor farmers. In the face of competing demands for scarce cash surpluses from agriculture, most manage their production risk through diversified farming systems, low-input utilization strategies, and off-farm income.

Too often, agricultural insurance is perceived by policy makers as a means by which to provide a safety net for farmers or even to increase their agricultural revenue. Agricultural insurance cannot solve problems of low farm income and poverty by itself. Although it can sometimes help channel additional social benefits to targeted farmers, it should not be considered an instrument that can provide poor farmers with higher revenues.

Agricultural insurance cannot replace sound financial practices. Although it can facilitate access to credit by reducing the default risk on loans caused by production shortfalls, it is not a substitute for sound financial discipline and financial risk management.

Policy Recommendations

Agriculture remains an important economic sector and a primary source of livelihood in many developing countries. A comprehensive agricultural risk management approach, including physical risk mitigation and financial risk management, can contribute to the modernization of the sector. Access to financial services—including agricultural insurance and other risk financing instruments, such as savings or (contingent) credit—can help farmers and herders engage in more productive farming practices and ensure that they can start a new production cycle after a natural disaster.

Agriculture insurance can contribute to the modernization of agriculture. However, it cannot operate in isolation. It should be promoted only when basic agricultural services—extension services, the timely availability of inputs, and efficient marketing channels for agricultural outputs—are in place.

Agricultural insurance can complement and enhance agricultural risk mitigation activities. It can protect farmers and herders against infrequent but severe adverse natural events that cannot be eliminated through cost-effective risk mitigation. Agricultural insurance can also be part of a climate change adaptation strategy, by, for example, facilitating access to credit linked to investment in climate-resilient farming activities.

Key policy recommendations can be derived from the review of agricultural insurance programs. These recommendations provide decision makers with some basic principles to consider in four areas: customization of agricultural programs, enhancement of agricultural insurance market through public-private partnerships, risk-based pricing, and targeted premium subsidies.

Customizing Agricultural Insurance Programs

Public multiple peril crop insurance (MPCI) programs designed in the 1970 and 1980s were aimed at providing universal coverage to all crops and all farmers. Their objective was to ensure a minimal level of economic security to farmers, particularly subsistence farmers involved in low-profitability activities. They relied mainly on (contingent) wealth-transfer instruments rather than risk sharing.

Agricultural insurance programs should be based on an appropriate market segmentation to address the specific needs of commercial, emerging commercial, and traditional (subsistence) farmers. This market segmentation is discussed below.

Market-based agricultural insurance is oriented toward viable business activities that generate adequate profits for the insured to be able to afford the insurance premium. These instruments, based on sound actuarial principles, should apply only to viable farms whose survival may be jeopardized by the occurrence of an insured event.

The commercial agricultural sector needs individual and tailor-made commercial insurance. Large and commercial specialized production units tend to be run on a purely commercial basis. They use expensive technology that requires intensive capitalization, which is financed by borrowed funds from the formal financial sector. Agricultural insurance is often an integral part of these enterprises' overall financial risk management strategy, complementing savings and credit.

The emerging commercial agricultural sector needs more standardized insurance products offered through cooperatives or rural finance institutions, such as credit-linked agricultural insurance. The sector includes small and medium-size enterprises that grow at least one commercial crop and derive a significant fraction of their household income from agriculture. Family labor is still predominant, although families often invest in production technology, such as hybrid seeds and fertilizer. Families in this sector are coming out of subsistence farming and just entering into commercial production. Agricultural insurance can complement other agricultural risk management activities (such as use of pesticides, irrigation), particularly by focusing on more severe but less frequent adverse natural events. Agricultural insurance can also facilitate access to credit to modernize their production systems.

The traditional farming sector mainly needs social safety net programs. It is characterized by a very large number of farmers operating small holdings using mainly family labor with limited use of purchased inputs. The primary goal of this sector is to meet subsistence requirements, not produce crops and livestock for sale. These farmers rarely borrow from the formal banking sector to invest in their agricultural business activity. Appropriate agricultural risk management measures, such as secure access to inputs and risk mitigation activities, must first be implemented before commercial insurance can become viable. However, as part of social safety net programs, governments may want to use insurance as a wealth-transfer mechanism when alternative public channels are inefficient.

Enhancing Market-Based Agricultural Insurance through Public-Private Partnerships

The public MPCI programs developed in the 1970s and 1980s have performed very poorly. In most cases, the shift from public to private agricultural insurance, usually through public-private partnerships, has led to more accountability and improved financial performance in agricultural insurance programs. As the survey results show, however, there is still room for improvement.

Agricultural insurance is a complex line of business that requires highly technical expertise, in both the development and the operational phases. It can expose insurers to major losses because of the systemic component of most agricultural production risks. Private insurance markets have proved to be efficient for dealing with nonsystemic risk (such as hail) and large farmers; purely commercial insurance may not be viable for systemic risks or smaller farmers.

The primary role of government should be to address market and regulatory imperfections in order to encourage participation by the private insurance sector. Government should focus mainly on developing risk market infrastructure, such as a strong and enabling regulatory framework, public awareness campaigns, data collection and management, and capacity building. Some countries have developed a regulatory framework for agricultural insurance, usually under their non–life insurance regulation. Public regulatory activities are well developed in only a few countries, however, such as Mexico and Spain.

Public intervention can be justified on two grounds. First, it is possible that the top risk layers cannot be efficiently placed in the private reinsurance market. Government intervention in these cases would complement the private reinsurance capacity. This form of catastrophe reinsurance is available in Kazakhstan, Mexico, and Spain. Second, in some countries, such as Mongolia, agricultural insurance is not mature enough to attract international private reinsurance. In such cases, the government can act as the sole reinsurer.

Using Risk-Based Price Signals to Encourage Sound Financial Planning and Risk Mitigation

In competitive markets, insurance premiums should be risk based and differentiated, reflecting the underlying risk exposure. Actuarially sound rates draw attention to the agricultural production risk exposure of individuals, firms, and governments and allow them to evaluate the benefits of agricultural risk management programs by comparing the cost of risk reduction investments with the resulting reduction in potential losses. They inform farmers and herders about their risk exposure and provide them with incentives to invest in risk mitigation activities (such as irrigation) or shift from nonviable crops to more viable crops.

Risk-based premiums can also assist governments in budgeting for agricultural losses by helping them assess their contingent liability. By understanding their exposure, governments can better assess their liabilities in the event of natural calamities and devise appropriate financial strategies.

Targeting Subsidies of Public Agricultural Insurance

Governments should carefully analyze the fiscal implications of government-sponsored agricultural insurance programs. The World Bank survey of

65 countries suggests that the (upfront) cost to the government of providing premium subsidies is about 44 percent of the original gross premium. Including administrative and operating and claim subsidies, the total cost to the government of providing agricultural insurance may be as high as 68 percent of original gross premiums. Such expensive public subsidy programs can place a major financial burden on governments, particularly in low- and middle-income countries. Moreover, provision of subsidies can distort price signals and provide inappropriate incentives to farmers and herders to invest in unprofitable or excessively risky farming activities.

Subsidizing insurance premiums can be justified to correct and promote competitive private agricultural insurance markets, usually in the form of public goods that enhance the risk market infrastructure (for example, data collection and management, research and development, and legal and regulatory framework). Subsidies on social insurance premiums act as a wealth-transfer mechanism. They are part of social safety net programs to ensure minimum incomes to farmers involved in unviable farming activities. Agricultural insurance can be used to provide this assistance when public channels are known to be inefficient.

The World Bank survey does not support the argument that premium subsidies are always necessary to induce farmers and livestock breeders to purchase crop and livestock insurance. Affordability of premiums is linked both to the riskiness of the enterprise and to the profit margin. The survey results show that in countries with a strong tradition of agricultural insurance, penetration rates for named-peril crop and livestock insurance are just as high as those for insurance that is highly subsidized. The challenge thus appears to be to design and rate products that meet farmers' real risk exposures and risk-transfer requirements.

Key Challenges and Options

Governments promoting or enhancing agricultural insurance will face institutional, financial, technical, and operational challenges. Each of these challenges and potential solutions is discussed below.

Institutional Challenges

Governments face major institutional challenges in promoting agricultural insurance. Public-private partnerships require an enabling regulatory framework. Agricultural insurance also should complement other technical and financial services that help farmers improve their practices.

Promoting market-based agricultural insurance. An appropriate institutional framework for agricultural insurance has proved critical for the emergence of sustainable agricultural insurance. Most public sector MPCI programs developed in the 1970s and 1980s have performed very poorly. The shift in the 1990s to market-based agricultural insurance has marked a renewal of interest in agricultural insurance. Governments should create an enabling environment for the development of private agricultural insurance. Their main role should be to correct any market imperfections that could hamper the emergence of a competitive private insurance market.

Facilitating access to technical and financial assistance. Agricultural insurance pools can be justified when domestic insurers have neither the technical nor the financial capacity to underwrite agricultural insurance. Pools can facilitate access to technical and financial assistance, sometimes provided by governments. In Turkey, for example, agricultural pools enabled domestic insurers to implement common underwriting and loss assessment standards and to improve the terms on which they accessed international agricultural reinsurance markets.

Promoting an enabling legal and regulatory framework. Although there are some differences between agricultural insurance and other forms of insurance, the general principles governing the regulation and supervision of insurance and insurance contracts are largely applicable to agricultural insurance. Best practice therefore suggests that general insurance law should be applied to agricultural insurance, allowing for different provisions to be made for agricultural insurance where appropriate. The legal and regulatory framework should also allow index-based insurance, such as weather-based crop insurance, to be classified as insurance products when there is a reasonable correlation between the index and the insured's loss. Insurance law could also allow, under proper supervision, cooperatives or financial institutions such as microfinance institutions to act as insurance agents and eventually to retain some risks and pass excess risk to the insurance industry.

Integrating agricultural insurance for small and marginal farmers with other products and services. World Bank experience in Bangladesh, India, Malawi, Senegal, and elsewhere shows that agricultural insurance cannot operate in isolation and that it often ranks very low on the list of priorities of small and marginal farmers and herders. Crop producers' priorities are first to ensure that they have timely access to inputs of seeds, fertilizers, and often credit with which to buy these inputs. Only then can they consider purchasing crop insurance. In Malawi crop weather index insurance is bundled with financial services (credit), input supply (seeds and fertilizer), and intensive farmer education and training as well as a strong output marketing organization. Livestock mortality insurance in Bangladesh and India has been successful where it has been complemented by livestock vaccination programs and intensive support and training in improved livestock husbandry and management, all of which reduce livestock mortality rates.

Promoting voluntary insurance. Voluntary private sector agricultural insurance has replaced compulsory public sector programs that operated throughout the Soviet Union and in much of Latin America. This model should be promoted. In special circumstances (including epidemic diseases in livestock), there may be a strong case for compulsory insurance for all livestock producers, as practiced in Netherlands, Switzerland, and de facto China for epidemic diseases in swine. For catastrophe windstorm and flood insurance, there may also be circumstances in which compulsory insurance is the only way to achieve adequate spread of risk. This applies particularly for specialized insurance programs, such as the Wincrop banana insurance program in the Windward Islands, which requires all banana growers to join the windstorm insurance program across four islands; their risks are pooled and then reinsured under a single excess-of-loss insurance and reinsurance program. Mauritius' sugar fund also requires mandatory agricultural insurance cover.

Financial Challenges

Governments should promote a cost-effective risk layering of agricultural production risks, in which small and recurrent risks are retained by farmers or groups of farmers, less frequent but more severe losses are transferred to the domestic insurance industry, and catastrophic losses are transferred to the international reinsurance market, possibly backed by governments. Governments can help domestic insurance companies pool their agricultural risks into more diversified and better-structured portfolios before approaching international reinsurance markets. Agricultural insurance pools can aggregate risk, insulating agricultural risks from other lines of business, particularly in low-income countries, where the domestic insurance industry may have limited capital to sustain catastrophic agricultural losses. Agricultural insurance pools are operating in Mongolia, Spain, and Turkey. This model is particularly appropriate for low-income countries in which the insurance industry is underdeveloped.

Where private reinsurance is too expensive or not available, governments can complement private reinsurance for top risk layers. They can act as reinsurers or lenders of last resort through contingent loans. They can play an important role in supporting reinsurance programs, as they do in one-third of the survey countries, including China, Mexico, Spain, and the United States.

Governments should rethink the role of agricultural premium subsidies. Where they use premium subsidies to promote agricultural insurance, most use a single flat-rate premium subsidy, usually on the order of 50 percent of the premium. A single premium subsidy level is a very blunt policy instrument with which to promote agricultural insurance to specific target groups, for specific crops, in specific regions. Some countries, including Costa Rica, Portugal, and Spain, have developed variable premium rates for different types of farmers, crops, and regions. Other countries could consider modifying their premium subsidy programs along similar lines.

Technical Challenges

Thorough risk assessment, linked to ongoing product development, is a precondition for the development of sustainable agricultural insurance.

Risk assessment that analyzes and quantifies production risks is a critical first step in trying to improve agricultural risk management in developing countries.

Catastrophe modeling offers new tools with which to assess the economic impact of extreme weather events. Very often, production risks and their financial impacts are underestimated or misdiagnosed, leading to interventions that are inappropriate and ineffective. The government should promote the development of catastrophe risk models and other risk assessment tools.

Governments should grant insurers access to reliable and timely agricultural and weather data, which allow them to properly assess the underlying agricultural risks and design and price actuarially sound insurance products. The role of national statistical offices is essential in collecting agricultural data, not only for policy purposes but also for insurance purposes. The weather department also plays a central role in providing weather data to the insurance industry. A relatively dense network of tamper-proof weather stations is essential to the development of weather index insurance products.

Governments should support research and development into innovative agricultural insurance products and services. Many emerging markets still severely overrely on standard MPCI covers for all crops, farmers, and regions. A need exists to develop alternative named-peril and index-based products. Governments can play an important role in assisting private sector crop insurers by financing research and development into new products and programs. Mexico is a good example of a middle-income country in which major investments have been made by both the public insurance institution (Agroasemex) and private insurers in developing a wide range of crop (and livestock) insurance products to fit different circumstances. In contrast, in Kazakhstan and Paraguay, where crop insurance is very new and all insurers underwrite a standard MPCI policy for cereals, catastrophe drought-related losses have jeopardized the viability of crop insurance.

The development of agricultural insurance is a long-term effort. International experience shows that it takes a long time to develop a comprehensive series of sustainable agricultural insurance products that are attractive to farmers. After more than 50 years of operations, the

U.S. agricultural insurance program still overrelies on a costly MPCI program, and livestock insurance remains underdeveloped. Spain's program has been implemented for more than 30 years, and new products are still tested annually. Governments should carefully design and pilot agricultural insurance programs before expanding them nationwide. International experience shows that it takes about three to five years of piloting before a program is ready for scaling up.

Particular attention should be given to the development of products for small and marginal farmers. MPCI programs have been implemented in several developing countries with limited success. Such products are complex and require heavy monitoring in order to mitigate moral hazard and adverse selection. They are therefore poorly suited to the needs of small and marginal farmers. Instead, innovative products such as index-based insurance as well as alternative delivery channels, such as rural banks and farmers groups, should be promoted.

Agricultural insurance products should be tailored to the targeted clients. Universal programs have proved to be inefficient: there is no "one size fits all" solution. Insurance policies should be designed to reflect the perils and types of farmers/herders to be protected. In particular, the following lessons should be applied:

- MPCI is efficient when the insurer can closely monitor farming practices and agricultural production risks are minimized through risk mitigation activities. These criteria are met mainly by large commercial farms that control their risk exposure.

- Named-peril crop insurance has proven to be commercially viable, because the insured peril is well identified and losses are relatively easy to assess through simple and objective systems of adjustment.

- Area-yield crop insurance is best suited to crops and hazard combinations for which a series of more complex perils simultaneously affects a crop in a particular region. It requires an efficient crop yield sampling and loss adjustment system.

- Weather-based crop insurance offers some promise, but only for selected hazards, such as drought or frost, which have a direct and simple impact on crop yield losses. Effective weather-based crop insurance products are difficult to design if losses are caused by a complex interaction among multiple weather variables.

- Livestock insurance faces the same challenges as crop insurance. Livestock accident and mortality insurance is effective when combined with veterinary services. Epidemic diseases are more difficult to cover, because they can cause catastrophic losses.

Governments should facilitate access to best practices in agricultural insurance rate-making. Agricultural insurance rating is critical to the sustainability of agricultural insurance. Actuarially sound rate-making techniques, such as the experience-based approach and credibility theory, should be promoted.

Operational Challenges

Operational procedures in agricultural insurance are complex and require specific expertise. Governments should facilitate access to international good practice on agricultural insurance underwriting, agricultural insurance policy terms and conditions, loss adjustment procedures, and so forth. Operational manuals could be drafted with the assistance of international agricultural reinsurers and, if necessary, with support from the donor community.

Loss assessment procedures can be complex and expensive, and they are often crop specific. Indemnity-based insurance is viable when the insurance company can discriminate between policyholders (to avoid adverse selection) and monitor them (to avoid moral hazard). Loss adjustment procedures can be expensive and require close supervision. These products are suited for well-defined perils (such as hail) and large farms (that is, cases in which monitoring costs are acceptable relative to premiums). Index-based insurance can partly avoid informational asymmetries and does not require individual loss adjustment, but it exposes the policyholder to basis risk (risk associated with the imperfect correlation between the actual loss and the index). Delivering and servicing agricultural insurance in rural areas, particularly to scattered small and marginal farmers, can be very expensive and significantly affect the commercial premium. These costs can be high whatever type of insurance is offered (indemnity based or index based). Governments should promote the role of intermediaries (marketing groups, cooperatives, banks, mutual groups) that can aggregate clients and risks and service the products at low costs.

Cooperatives, producer associations, rural banks, and microfinance institutions can play an important and cost-effective role in delivering crop and livestock insurance products and services to small farmers. In Asian countries such as Bangladesh, India, Nepal, and the Philippines, cooperatives, other forms of community-based organization, and microfinance institutions with very large rural memberships are delivering a range of financial products (microcredit) and sometimes microinsurance (usually life and health insurance) to their members. They operate as distributing agents for products underwritten by local insurance companies (under a partner-agent model) or under some form of mutual insurance or partner insurance model. These insurance and delivery channels operate at very low overhead costs compared with private commercial insurance companies and could form the basis for future development and scaling up of agricultural insurance provision.

Local insurance legislation does not formally recognize most of these community-based and mutual insurance schemes (except for those based on the partner-agent model), and such mechanisms are not usually able to attract reinsurance protection. Given that they offer new opportunities for providing agricultural insurance, they have received too little attention by policy makers and planners.

In start-up situations where market infrastructure is not yet developed, a technical support unit could be established to provide specialized services to agricultural insurance companies and other risk-pooling vehicles. This unit should have support from the government, insurers, and reinsurers. Technical support could be provided either by a stand-alone entity or by an insurance provider (such as agricultural insurance pools or a monopoly insurer). Such support could aim to achieve the following:

- Create a center of expertise able to support the development and scaling up of agricultural insurance.

- Establish a core team of agricultural insurance experts to provide technical support to agricultural insurers in underwriting, product development, pricing, product delivery, loss adjustment, catastrophe risk financing, and other facets of insurance provision

- Create and manage a centralized database of agricultural statistics and weather statistics, and make it available to agricultural insurance practitioners.

- Promote the exchange of expertise among insurance companies and access to international best practice through training courses, operations manuals, and other means.

Status of Agricultural Insurance in 209 Economies

Table A.1 Status of Agricultural Insurance, by Economy, 2008

Economy	Income group	Agricultural insurance offered in country
Afghanistan	Low-income	No
Albania	Lower-middle-income	Unknown
Algeria	Lower-middle-income	Pilot
American Samoa	Upper-middle-income	Unknown
Andorra	High-income	Yes
Angola	Lower-middle-income	No
Antigua and Barbuda	High-income	No
Argentina	Upper-middle-income	Yes
Armenia	Lower-middle-income	No
Aruba	High-income	No
Australia	High-income	Yes
Austria	High-income	Yes
Azerbaijan	Lower-middle-income	Yes
Bahamas, The	High-income	No
Bahrain	High-income	No
Bangladesh	Low-income	Yes
Barbados	High-income	Unknown
Belarus	Upper-middle-income	Unknown
Belgium	High-income	Yes
Belize	Upper-middle-income	Unknown
Benin	Low-income	No
Bermuda	High-income	No
Bhutan	Lower-middle-income	No

(continued)

Table A.1 Status of Agricultural Insurance, by Economy, 2008 *(continued)*

Economy	Income group	Agricultural insurance offered in country
Bolivia, Plurinational State of	Lower-middle-income	Pilot
Bosnia and Herzegovina	Lower-middle-income	Unknown
Botswana	Upper-middle-income	No
Brazil	Upper-middle-income	Yes
Brunei Darussalam	High-income	No
Bulgaria	Upper-middle-income	Yes
Burkina Faso	Low-income	No
Burundi	Low-income	No
Cambodia	Low-income	No
Cameroon	Lower-middle-income	Unknown
Canada	High-income	Yes
Cape Verde	Lower-middle-income	No
Cayman Islands	High-income	No
Central African Republic	Low-income	No
Chad	Low-income	Unknown
Channel Islands	High-income	Unknown
Chile	Upper-middle-income	Yes
China	Lower-middle-income	Yes
Colombia	Lower-middle-income	Yes
Comoros	Low-income	No
Congo, Dem. Rep.	Low-income	No
Congo, Rep.	Lower-middle-income	No
Costa Rica	Upper-middle-income	Yes
Côte d'Ivoire	Low-income	Unknown
Croatia	Upper-middle-income	Unknown
Cuba	Upper-middle-income	Yes
Cyprus	High-income	Yes
Czech Republic	High-income	Yes
Denmark	High-income	Yes
Djibouti	Lower-middle-income	No
Dominica	Upper-middle-income	Yes
Dominican Republic	Lower-middle-income	Yes
Ecuador	Lower-middle-income	Yes
Egypt, Arab Rep. of	Lower-middle-income	Unknown
El Salvador	Lower-middle-income	Pilot
Equatorial Guinea	High-income	Unknown
Eritrea	Low-income	Unknown
Estonia	High-income	Yes
Ethiopia	Low-income	Pilot
Faeroe Islands	High-income	Yes
Fiji	Upper-middle-income	Unknown
Finland	High-income	Yes

(continued)

Table A.1 Status of Agricultural Insurance, by Economy, 2008 *(continued)*

Economy	Income group	Agricultural insurance offered in country
France	High-income	Yes
French Polynesia	High-income	Yes
Gabon	Upper-middle-income	Unknown
Gambia, The	Low-income	Unknown
Georgia	Lower-middle-income	Unknown
Germany	High-income	Yes
Ghana	Low-income	Unknown
Greece	High-income	Yes
Greenland	High-income	Unknown
Grenada	Upper-middle-income	Yes
Guam	High-income	Yes
Guatemala	Lower-middle-income	Pilot
Guinea	Low-income	Unknown
Guinea-Bissau	Low-income	Unknown
Guyana	Lower-middle-income	No
Haiti	Low-income	No
Honduras	Lower-middle-income	Yes
Hong Kong, China	High-income	Yes
Hungary	High-income	Yes
Iceland	High-income	Unknown
India	Lower-middle-income	Yes
Indonesia	Lower-middle-income	Yes
Iran, Islamic Rep. of	Lower-middle-income	Yes
Iraq	Lower-middle-income	No
Ireland	High-income	Yes
Isle of Man	High-income	Unknown
Israel	High-income	Yes
Italy	High-income	Yes
Jamaica	Upper-middle-income	Yes
Japan	High-income	Yes
Jordan	Lower-middle-income	Unknown
Kazakhstan	Upper-middle-income	Yes
Kenya	Low-income	Pilot
Kiribati	Lower-middle-income	No
Korea, Dem. Rep. of	Low-income	Yes
Korea, Rep. of	High-income	Yes
Kuwait	High-income	Unknown
Kyrgyz Republic	Low-income	Unknown
Lao PDR	Low-income	No
Latvia	Upper-middle-income	Yes
Lebanon	Upper-middle-income	Unknown
Lesotho	Lower-middle-income	No

(continued)

Table A.1 Status of Agricultural Insurance, by Economy, 2008 *(continued)*

Economy	Income group	Agricultural insurance offered in country
Liberia	Low-income	Unknown
Libya	Upper-middle-income	Unknown
Liechtenstein	High-income	Unknown
Lithuania	Upper-middle-income	Yes
Luxembourg	High-income	Yes
Macao, China	High-income	Unknown
Macedonia, FYR	Lower-middle-income	Unknown
Madagascar	Low-income	No
Malawi	Low income	Pilot
Malaysia	Upper-middle-income	Yes
Maldives	Lower-middle-income	No
Mali	Low-income	No
Malta	High-income	Unknown
Marshall Islands	Lower-middle-income	Unknown
Mauritania	Low-income	No
Mauritius	Upper-middle-income	Yes
Mayotte	Upper-middle-income	Unknown
Mexico	Upper-middle-income	Yes
Micronesia, Fed. Sts.	Lower-middle-income	No
Moldova	Lower-middle-income	Yes
Monaco	High-income	No
Mongolia	Lower-middle-income	Pilot
Montenegro	Upper-middle-income	Yes
Morocco	Lower-middle-income	Yes
Mozambique	Low-income	No
Myanmar	Low-income	No
Namibia	Lower-middle-income	Unknown
Nepal	Low-income	Yes
Netherlands	High-income	Yes
Netherlands Antilles	High-income	Unknown
New Caledonia	High-income	Unknown
New Zealand	High-income	Yes
Nicaragua	Lower-middle-income	Pilot
Niger	Low-income	No
Nigeria	Low-income	Yes
Northern Mariana Islands	High-income	Unknown
Norway	High-income	Yes
Oman	High-income	Yes
Pakistan	Low-income	Pilot
Palau	Upper-middle-income	No
Panama	Upper-middle-income	Yes
Papua New Guinea	Low-income	No

(continued)

Table A.1 Status of Agricultural Insurance, by Economy, 2008 *(continued)*

Economy	Income group	Agricultural insurance offered in country
Paraguay	Lower-middle-income	Yes
Peru	Lower-middle-income	Pilot
Philippines	Lower-middle-income	Yes
Poland	Upper-middle-income	Yes
Portugal	High-income	Yes
Puerto Rico	High-income	Yes
Qatar	High income	Pilot
Romania	Upper-middle-income	Yes
Russian Federation	Upper-middle-income	Yes
Rwanda	Low-income	No
Samoa	Lower-middle-income	No
San Marino	High-income	Unknown
São Tomé and Principe	Low-income	Unknown
Saudi Arabia	High-income	Pilot
Senegal	Low-income	Pilot
Serbia	Upper-middle-income	Yes
Seychelles	Upper-middle-income	No
Sierra Leone	Low-income	No
Singapore	High-income	Yes
Slovak Republic	High-income	Yes
Slovenia	High-income	Yes
Solomon Islands	Low-income	No
Somalia	Low-income	No
South Africa	Upper-middle-income	Yes
Spain	High-income	Yes
Sri Lanka	Lower-middle-income	Yes
St. Kitts and Nevis	Upper-middle-income	No
St. Lucia	Upper-middle-income	Yes
St. Vincent and the Grenadines	Upper-middle-income	Yes
Sudan	Lower-middle-income	Yes
Suriname	Upper middle income	Unknown
Swaziland	Lower-middle-income	Unknown
Sweden	High-income	Yes
Switzerland	High-income	Yes
Syrian Arab Rep.	Lower-middle-income	Unknown
Tajikistan	Low-income	Unknown
Tanzania	Low-income	Pilot
Thailand	Lower-middle-income	Pilot
Timor-Leste	Lower-middle-income	Unknown
Togo	Low-income	Unknown
Tonga	Lower-middle-income	Unknown
Trinidad and Tobago	High-income	Unknown

(continued)

Table A.1 Status of Agricultural Insurance, by Economy, 2008 *(continued)*

Economy	Income group	Agricultural insurance offered in country
Tunisia	Lower-middle-income	Yes
Turkey	Upper-middle-income	Yes
Turkmenistan	Lower-middle-income	Unknown
Uganda	Low-income	Pilot
Ukraine	Lower-middle-income	Yes
United Arab Emirates	High-income	Unknown
United Kingdom	High-income	Yes
United States	High-income	Yes
Uruguay	Upper-middle-income	Yes
Uzbekistan	Low-income	Unknown
Vanuatu	Lower-middle-income	No
Venezuela, R. B. de	Upper-middle-income	Yes
Vietnam	Low-income	Pilot
Virgin Islands (U.S.)	High-income	Unknown
West Bank and Gaza	Lower-middle-income	Unknown
Yemen, Rep.	Low-income	Unknown
Zambia	Low-income	Unknown
Zimbabwe	Low-income	Unknown

Source: World Bank List of Economies (July 2008) ; World Bank Survey 2008.
Note: The World Bank divides all economies into income groups based on 2008 per capita gross national income (GNI), calculated using the World Bank Atlas method. Through July 1, 2009, the classifications were as follows: low-income: $975 or less; lower-middle-income: $976–$3,855; upper-middle-income: $3,856–$11,905; high-income: $11,906 or more.

Financial Management of Agricultural Production Risks

T raditional subsidized agricultural insurance programs are not sustainable in the long run, especially in low-income countries that face fiscal constraints. The World Bank is therefore promoting a proactive and strategic approach for the financial management of agricultural production risks. Its model should be implemented only after cost-effective risk mitigation techniques (such as irrigation and pesticides) have been implemented. The proposed model thus deals only with the residual risk that cannot be mitigated.

The country agricultural risk financing model is based on four pillars. It offers countries an operational template with which to implement a financially sustainable agricultural insurance program (figure B.1).

Decomposition of Agribusiness Segments

The inherent lack of clarity regarding the objectives of public intervention in agricultural insurance has contributed to its inefficiencies. Social insurance, or safety nets, aims to ensure a minimal level of economic security to all farmers, particularly those involved in low-profit activities. These social objectives rely on (contingent) wealth-transfer instruments.

Market-based insurance is oriented toward business activities that generate enough profit to pay for insurance premiums. These instruments,

Figure B.1 Financial Management of Agriculture Risk

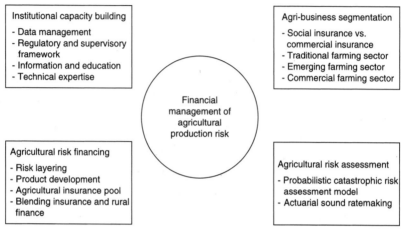

Institutional capacity building	Agri-business segmentation
- Data management - Regulatory and supervisory framework - Information and education - Technical expertise	- Social insurance vs. commercial insurance - Traditional farming sector - Emerging farming sector - Commercial farming sector

Financial management of agricultural production risk

Agricultural risk financing	Agricultural risk assessment
- Risk layering - Product development - Agricultural insurance pool - Blending insurance and rural finance	- Probabilistic catastrophic risk assessment model - Actuarial sound ratemaking

Source: Authors.

based on sound actuarial principles, should apply only to viable farms whose survival may be jeopardized by the occurrence of an insured event. The farming sector can be decomposed into three categories, each of which has specific agricultural insurance needs.

- *The traditional farming sector.* This sector includes a very large number of farmers operating small holdings using mainly family labor with limited use of artificial inputs such as fertilizers and other agrochemicals. These farmers are rarely able to borrow from the formal banking sector to invest in their agricultural business activity. They produce primarily for home consumption, although in good seasons they may sell their surplus in the market. Nonfarm income represents a large fraction of total household income. The preconditions for developing commercial agricultural insurance are missing in this sector.

- *The semicommercial and emerging commercial sector.* This sector includes medium-size holdings that grow at least one commercial crop and derive a significant fraction of their household income from agriculture. Family labor is predominant. Farmers invest in production technology, such as hybrid seeds and fertilizer. They are coming out of mere subsistence farming and entering into commercial production. Agriculture insurance could improve their viability by providing external capital to finance infrequent agricultural shocks. However, traditional insurance may be unviable, because of high transactions costs relative to the level of liability. Standardized index-based insurance products (such as insurance based on area yield or rainfall), offered through cooperatives or rural finance institutions, may be appropriate for this sector.

- *The commercial sector.* This sector includes large and commercial specialized production units run on a purely commercial basis. Individual enterprises are commercially viable and have large asset bases. Farmers generally prepare gross margin budgets in advance, which provide a starting point for evaluating enterprise viability. They use expensive technology that requires intensive capitalization, which they finance with funds borrowed from the formal financial sector. These agricultural business units need individual and tailor-made insurance products.

Experience shows that the demand for risk management instruments is usually low or even nonexistent among farmers who do not borrow for investment purposes. In contrast, farmers who borrow have more incentives to purchase risk management instruments, either because the banks require them to be insured or because these products allow them to access credit at better terms. Credit-linked risk management instruments should thus be the first type of product promoted.

Agricultural Risk Assessment

One of the main reasons why agricultural insurance has so far been underdeveloped worldwide is the complexity of risk and the lack of adequate risk-modeling technology to understand the impact of agricultural risks, particularly drought, on crop yields. Catastrophe modeling is an evolving science that aids policymakers and other stakeholders in managing the risk from natural disasters. Models focus mainly on the impact of rapid-onset disasters (for example, earthquakes, hurricanes, floods) on public or private infrastructure. This risk assessment paradigm must be adapted to slow-onset disasters (for example, drought).

The World Bank recently developed and tested a probabilistic drought risk assessment model in India. This stochastic agro-meteorological model offers policymakers a powerful tool with which to better understand the consequences of drought in the different sectors of the economy, quantify such impacts with respect to the drought severity, and investigate the economic impacts of risk coping strategies, at both the farm and state levels. The stochastic dimension included in this model also allows policymakers to capture the underlying uncertainty related to weather events, including the impact of anticipated permanent changes in climate. This model offers opportunities to revisit agricultural insurance through catastrophic risk-modeling techniques.

Actuarially sound rate-making techniques should be used to price agricultural insurance products, in order to ensure their sustainability and cost-effectiveness. The World Bank has helped the Indian public crop insurance company—the Agricultural Insurance Company of India, Ltd. (AICI)—revise the rate-making methodology of the National Agricultural Insurance Scheme (NAIS) (the largest crop insurance scheme in the world, with about 20 million farmers insured every year) and the weather-based crop insurance scheme.

Agricultural Risk Financing

Agricultural risk financing relies on optimally layering agricultural risks, with each risk layer covered by specific financial instruments. Insurance pools can enhance the sustainability of agricultural insurance programs.

Risk Layering

Risk financing deals with the residual risks that cannot be mitigated with cost-effective preventive measures. They can be financed through an appropriate layering of risks by farmers' self-retention, private financial markets, governments, and international donors (figure B.2).

- The bottom layer of risk includes high-frequency (for example, occurring at least once every five years) but low-consequence risks that affect farmers from a variety of mainly independent risks. These losses may be caused by inappropriate management decisions and are thus exposed to moral hazard and adverse selection problems. These risks

Figure B.2 Layering of Agricultural Production Risk

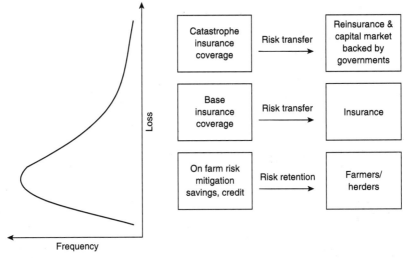

Source: Authors.

should be retained by farmers and herders and financed by individual savings and credit.

- The mezzanine layer of risk includes less frequent (for example, occurring one to six times every 30 years) but more severe risks that affect many farmers at the same time (for example, hail, frost). The private insurance industry has demonstrated its ability to cover these losses. However, this base insurance coverage may expose the insurance industry to aggregate insured losses. It may want to transfer these excessive losses through reinsurance.

- The top layer of risk includes low-frequency (for example, occurring once every 20 years or less) but high-severity risks. These catastrophic risks are by definition not well documented, and the probable maximum loss can be very large. The cost of transferring these risks (that is, the insurance premium) can be high compared with the annual average loss, making reinsurance a costly risk financing mechanism. In addition, farmers are usually unwilling to purchase this insurance, because they tend to underestimate their exposure to catastrophic risks (cognitive failure) and rely on postdisaster emergency relief. Governments should cover these very infrequent losses through catastrophe insurance coverage as part of a social disaster relief program. Innovative financial products (for example, catastrophe bonds, catastrophe options, contingent debt) may offer new risk-transfer opportunities to the insurance markets and governments.

Product Development

Traditional insurance based on individual indemnities has proved to be unsustainable in developing countries, except for large-scale farmers and specific perils (such as hail and frost). Crop insurance solutions for small and medium-size farmers should therefore be based on indexes, such as area yield, rainfall, and temperature indexes.

Index-based insurance is an alternative form of insurance that makes payments based on an index, irrespective of individual losses. It offers advantages over traditional individual insurance (reduced moral hazard and adverse selection, low administrative costs, standardized product), but it exposes the insured to imperfect indemnification (that is, the possibility that the payout is different from the individual loss [basis risk]).

Although weather derivatives have been used primarily in the energy sector, the potential market for these instruments in agriculture is significant. Weather-based crop insurance products are currently offered in a few developed countries (Canada, the United States) and developing countries (India, Malawi, Mexico), mainly on a pilot basis.

The effectiveness of the weather insurance contract and its likely acceptance by farmers is determined by the extent to which the index reflects their individual losses. For a farmer with yields that are poorly related to the index, the index-based plan will provide little protection against yield risks. In Mongolia, for example, the complexity of the *dzud* (a dry summer followed by a harsh winter that causes the starvation and death of livestock) and the underfunded meteorological network ruled out the use of weather indexes. Policy makers therefore decided to use local livestock mortality rates (available for the past 30 years through the annual animal census) to design an insurance product that pays out whenever the adult mortality rate (as reported in the annual animal census) exceeds a specific threshold for a localized region. This product is simpler than weather-based insurance and less prone to moral hazard, adverse selection, and high administrative costs than individual insurance.

Satellite imagery offers new opportunities for agricultural insurance. The new generation of crop index-based insurance products will be based on the combination of historical ground data and high-precision earth observation remote-sensing real time data. The use of advanced remote-sensing satellite technology for insurance underwriting and monitoring purposes provides independent, reliable information about field sizes, date of sowing, crop yield measurement at time of harvest, and so forth. The first agricultural insurance program based on this technology is the pasture satellite imagery insurance program in Canada, launched in 2001. Use of this technology in the development of agricultural insurance programs is under investigation in some developing countries.

Agricultural Insurance Pool

Domestic insurance markets are underdeveloped in many developing countries. They lack both technical and financial capacity. In this context, agricultural insurance, as a new line of business, may expose them to an unacceptable level of risk that may affect the financial viability of the whole industry. It may be necessary to reinforce this line of business to protect the domestic insurance industry against a financial contagion caused by excessive agricultural insured losses.

An agricultural insurance pool could act as a risk aggregator, providing farmers and herders with affordable and effective agricultural insurance that is financially sustainable in the long term without heavy public subsidies (figure B.3). This model relies on a strong partnership between the government and domestic and international reinsurance markets. It is based on the World Bank's experience in Turkey (the Turkish Catastrophe Insurance Pool [TCIP]), the Caribbean (the Caribbean Catastrophe Risk Insurance Facility [CCRIF]), and Mongolia (the Mongolia Livestock Insurance Indemnity Pool). This pool should first propose standardized contracts covering specific risks (for example, floods, lack of rainfall) in order to limit transactions costs and adverse selection problems. Domestic insurance companies could act as agents, bringing the business to the pool in exchange for a commission, or they could buy shares of the pool based on their market shares. The risk capital of the pool could be provided either by the reinsurance market (through indemnity or index-based

Figure B.3 National Agricultural Insurance Pool

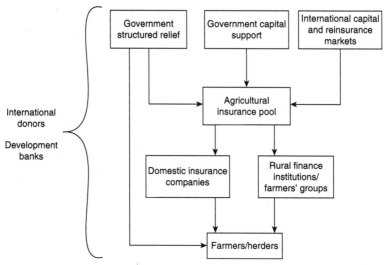

Source: Authors.

reinsurance, such as excess-of-loss reinsurance) or by the capital market (through risk securitization), thus facilitating access to the financial capacity of the asset markets.

This syndicated pooling arrangement would aim at facilitating, through a public-private partnership, the development of market-based agricultural insurance products. The key objectives to be achieved would be the following:

- Provide affordable and effective agricultural insurance coverage.

- Ensure that farmers receive full indemnity payments due (no default risk).

- Insulate the domestic insurance industry from catastrophic losses in this line of business.

- Act as a center of technical excellence to support small insurers.

- Provide the insurance industry with incentives to collaborate on the integrity of the program.

- Ensure efficient local retention by pooling nonretainable risks.

- Get optimal pricing from international reinsurers by providing a partly diversified portfolio.

- Limit government fiscal exposure.

Blending Insurance and Rural Finance

Rural finance institutions should play a central role in the financial management of agricultural production risks. By acting as insurance agents—marketing and selling insurance products to their clientele through the distribution network they have already established for their other financial services—they could reduce delivery costs. For rural finance institutions, the potential benefits of partnering include limited initial capital investment and low variable costs, rapid product launch, compliance with legal and regulatory requirements, stable revenue stream through commissions, business learning, and expansion of their financial services. The potential benefits for the insurance company include access to new markets, access to clientele with financial records, and lower transactions costs for serving new clients. The potential benefits for farmers include access to better products at a lower cost and the establishment of a strong, regulated local insurer. This model is particularly relevant, because credit-linked insurance should be the first insurance product to be promoted.

Rural finance institutions could use index-based insurance to hedge their portfolios of agricultural loans (for example, when drought is a major risk of default among farmers). By allowing them to transfer default risk, this hedging strategy would allow them to reduce the interest rates they charge their clients. This strategy has been pilot tested in India and is being investigated in Morocco and Peru.

Institutional Capacity Building

Governments, with the help of international institutions such as the World Bank, should create an economic and legal environment that facilitates the emergence of a competitive insurance market and provides farmers with incentives to engage in risk-financing strategies. This environment includes the following features:

- *Data management.* An efficient data management system is critical to the development of insurance products. It aims to build an accurate and complete historic database and to secure future data measurements from fraud and abuse.

- *Regulatory and supervisory framework.* A regulatory and supervisory framework is intended to ensure that insurers have the financial resources required to pay all claims as they become due and that they treat consumers in an equitable manner in all financial dealings. It is based on a set of rules that foster financial sector stability and public protection while ensuring market competitiveness and efficiency.

- *Risk financing entity.* Governments should contribute to the financing only of losses that cannot be transferred to the private market at acceptable costs. They should focus on catastrophic losses, acting as reinsurers of last resort, when the financial resources of the domestic insurance industry are scarce and access to international reinsurance markets is limited. This temporary risk arrangement should allow insurance companies to build up reserves and retain more risk over time. The resulting risk exposure of governments should be adequately financed through an appropriate country risk financing strategy, including, for example, reserve funds, reinsurance, and contingent debt facilities provided by international institutions such as the World Bank. The World Bank contingent debt facility is often less expensive than reinsurance for countries with an appropriate borrowing capacity, particularly for top-layer risks.

- *Information and education.* Information and education campaigns should be undertaken to reduce the widespread lack of insurance culture among farmers.

- *Technical expertise.* Agricultural insurance is a very technical field. At the top administrative level, it requires expertise in the design of the insurance scheme, the establishment of the terms and conditions of coverage, and the actuarial aspects of insurance. At the local level, there is a need for underwriters and personnel who can explain agricultural insurance to farmers and herders.

The Survey Questionnaire

Letter of Introduction

The letter of introduction shown below was sent to agricultural insurance insurers, brokers, and experts in more than 60 countries. It accompanied the survey questionnaire.

The World Bank INTERNATIONAL BANK FOR RECONSTRUCTION AND DEVELOPMENT INTERNATIONAL DEVELOPMENT ASSOCIATION	1818 H Street N.W. Washington, D.C. 20433 U.S.A.	(202) 473-1000 Cable Address: INTBAFRAD Cable Address: INDEVAS

April 8, 2008

<u>**To Whom It May Concern**</u>

Dear Sir/Madam,

World Bank Study on Public Intervention in Agriculture Insurance --
Request for Completing a Questionnaire

The World Bank has provided technical assistance on agricultural insurance to developing countries for more than a decade. Recent initiatives supported by the World Bank include weather based crop insurance in India, Malawi and Central America; index based livestock insurance in Mongolia; and area yield crop insurance in India. The World Bank assists governments to develop their policy towards agricultural insurance, including the establishment of public-private partnerships in agricultural insurance, in the context of improved ex ante planning against natural disasters.

RCA 248423. ⊡ WUI 64145 ⊡ FAX (202) 477-6391

- 2 -   April 8, 2008

Governments and national insurance associations in the developing countries are increasingly interested to support the emergence of agriculture insurance programs to help the farmers cope with the adverse events that affect their production. They are particularly eager to know how other countries have developed agriculture insurance programs, how governments have been involved in this process, and the lessons and recommendations that can be drawn from this experience. Unfortunately, this information is not always easily accessible.

In this context, the World Bank is conducting a study on *Public Intervention in Agricultural Insurance*. The purpose of this work is threefold: (i) discuss the rationale for public intervention in agricultural risk management; (ii) analyze the comparative performance of government sponsored agricultural insurance schemes and private un-subsidized agricultural insurance in selected countries; and (iii) propose guiding principles for public intervention in agricultural insurance in developing countries.

In particular, this study aims to collect the most recent and reliable information on selected agricultural insurance programs, including those offered in your country. To do so, a questionnaire has been developed to collect this information, and key persons within the agricultural insurance sector in each country have been identified. Several consultants have been appointed by the World Bank to coordinate the collection of data from specific countries, and this letter will be forwarded by the consultant who is responsible for your country.

I would be very grateful for your assistance towards this collaborative project. The gathering of relevant information is essential to the success of this study. **I would therefore be very grateful for your assistance in completing the attached questionnaire and returning it to the appointed consultant by May 5, 2008.** In return, we will be pleased to share with you the findings and conclusions of the World Bank study, to be released in November 2008, which will give you a worldwide perspective of the recent developments and trends in public intervention in agricultural insurance. Your contribution to the project will be acknowledged in the study.

Should you have any questions or concerns, please feel free to contact me directly.

I look forward to hearing from you.

Sincerely,

Olivier Mahul
Program Manager
Insurance for the Poor

Attachment

Contact Details:
Olivier Mahul
2121 Pennsylvania Avenue, NW
Washington DC, 20433
USA
Phone: (1) 202-458-8955
Email: omahul@worldbank.org

Explanatory Notes to Accompany Questionnaire on Public Intervention in Agricultural Insurance

The World Bank would be very appreciative of your assistance in completing this agricultural insurance questionnaire for your country

The Questionnaire is designed to be completed electronically and then e-mailed as an attached file to your Country Coordinator, whose contact details are given at the end of the guidance Notes

Most of the questions and requested statistics are intended to be answered at the "market level" for crop and livestock and other classes of agricultural insurance in your country. Where you do not have access to market-level agricultural insurance statistics, please complete the question(s) for your insurance company only.

The questionnaire

General:

There are 12 questions, which we would kindly ask you to complete as accurately as possible. For most questions, we include an additional comments section for you to add your own comments or observations

If it is easier for you to attach a table of figures that apply to a specific question, please append your tables at the end of the questionnaire or provide separately in an excel sheet

For most questions we distinguish between two major classes of agricultural insurance, namely, crops and livestock. We also refer to total agricultural insurance, which includes all crops and livestock and in addition forestry and aquaculture, as applicable in your country

Page 1 Respondent's name and Respondent's Insurance Company. Please advise if you do NOT want us to make any reference to your company in the World Bank's report.

Page 1 Country. Please name your country.

Province. If your company is a provincial agricultural insurer and you are completing the questionnaire only for that province, please state the name of the province.

Q.1 *When was agricultural insurance introduced in your country?* Please note the year when crop insurance and or livestock insurance was first introduced in your country.

Q.2 *Agricultural insurance market structure in 2007–08.* This question aims to provide a classification of the number and types of agricultural crop and livestock insurance companies in your country

For the purposes of this survey a "public sector insurer" is a company in which the government (national or provincial) has a majority shareholding. A "private sector insurer" has a majority shareholding with private investors. A coinsurance pool consists of two or more insurance companies that contractually agree to coinsure a crop insurance program and may consist of private and public insurance companies or private insurance companies only. The best-known example of a coinsurance pool is Spain's national agrarian insurance program, which is underwritten by the Agroseguro pool of public and private sector and mutual insurance companies.

Please list the number of companies in your market by type, and also note whether they underwrite crop only, or livestock only, or both crops and livestock.

Q.3 Agricultural Reinsurance Market

Q.3.1 *Are the crop and livestock programs in your country reinsured?* This is intended to be a market-based question as opposed to specific to individual insurance companies. If at least some insurance companies in your market purchase crop and/or livestock reinsurance (as applicable), please complete the questions in Q3.1. You may at the end comment on those companies that do not purchase crop or livestock (as applicable) reinsurance in your market

Q.3.2 *Access to private international agricultural insurance.* This is again intended as a market-level question, but if you do not have an overview, please complete for your company only (please tick appropriate box). For each class of agricultural insurance in the left-hand column, please indicate by ticking one box only whether access to private international reinsurance is no constraint, a moderate constraint, or finally a major constraint to development of that class of agricultural insurance.

Q.4 *Types of agricultural insurance product available through public and/or private insurance companies in 2007–08 (market-level question)*. This question is aimed at identifying the range of agricultural insurance product available through (a) public insurers (as identified in Q.2) and/or (b) private insurers (as identified in Q.2) in your country. For convenience, we have divided the products into two types: traditional indemnity-based products and index-based products. Area yield insurance is also termed group risk plan (GRP) in the United States. NDVI stands for normalized dry vegetative index, and RS refers to remote sensing.

Q.5 *Public sector support to agricultural insurance in 2007–08*

Q.5.1 *Form of government support to insurance.* We have identified a total of 11 forms or ways in which governments typically provide financial and other forms of assistance to the implementation of agricultural insurance. Please read this question carefully. IF there is no form of government support to agricultural crop or livestock insurance in your country, please pass to question 6.

If you have some form of government support in your country, please complete Questions 5.1–5.4. These are intended to be market-level questions as opposed to specific to your company only.

Q.5.2 *Who provides public sector agricultural insurance premium subsidies?* If government provides financial support in the form of premium subsidies (Q5.1.3), please complete Q5.2.

Q.5.3 *Premium subsidies for crops and livestock in 2007/2008?* If government provides financial support in the form of premium subsidies (Q5.1.3), please complete Q5.3.1–Q5.3.4. Please feel free to attach premium subsidy scales/tables under the appendices.

Q.5.4 *Costs to government of financial subsidies in last five years.* We are very interested in quantifying the costs of government financial support to agricultural crop and livestock insurance as per the five major headings (as applicable according to your responses in Q5.1) identified for crops, livestock, and then total agricultural insurance. Please make sure you specify the currency and units (for example, "€ '000"). In order for us to analyze change over time, please provide figures if possible for the past five years, starting with 2007 or the most recent year for which data are available.

Q.6 *Agricultural insurance delivery channels.* Please identify the main forms of crop and livestock delivery channel in your country by ranking each channel, starting with 1 as most important delivery channel (in terms of numbers of policy sales), 2 second most important, and so forth

Q.7 *Agricultural insurance participation (adoption) rates.* This question is aimed at analyzing changes in adoption rates of crop and livestock insurance over the past five years in your country at a national level

Crops. Please list for the past five years the number of crop insurance policies sold and provide estimates of the percentage of the total farmers in your country who purchase crop insurance Please also note the insured area in hectares for the past five years, and express this area as a percentage of the national arable cropped area in your country

Given the fact that uptake rates may be very different for different crop types in your country, please append any additional information on specific adoption/uptake rates for individual crops

Livestock. For livestock, please provide number of insured animals by type of animal, and express this as a percentage of the national herd for the most recent five years.

Q.8 *Agricultural insurance results past five years.* We are seeking whole market-level crop, livestock, and total agricultural insurance results over the past five years, including number of policies, total sum insured, total premium inclusive of premium subsidies if these apply, and paid claims. If whole market figures are not available, please provide us with your own company's results

Q.9 *Costs of agricultural insurance provision.* This question is aimed at quantifying the costs of agricultural crop and livestock insurance provision in your country. If specific information is not available through the insurance association, please provide estimates for your own company. We have identified four cost headings where we would ask you to express your average costs as a percentage of your original gross premium rate. For a crop or livestock department in a multiline insurance company, please calculate your administration costs on the basis of your departmental direct staff and operating costs and the share of overhead allocated from your general company.

Q.10 *Are there other forms of government support to agriculture, including disaster relief or natural catastrophe or epidemic disease compensation for crop and livestock producers?*

Please complete this question as fully as possible if in addition to crop and livestock insurance, there is any other form of government support to agriculture either in the form of a disaster relief program or natural catastrophe program.

Q.11 *Voluntary versus compulsory insurance.* Please provide details. We recognize that for some crops or livestock programs, insurance may be voluntary; for others it may be mandatory; for example, compulsory linkage of crop credit provision with crop insurance.

Q.12 *We highly value your personal opinion on the role of public sector intervention in agricultural insurance.* Please complete Q12 if you wish to add your own comments. Your responses will not be identified to you individually in our report.

Thank you for your assistance in this survey.

Please return the completed questionnaire to:

Name:
Email:
Tel:

Mailing address for hard copy if e-mail not possible:

Name:
Address:

Questionnaire

PUBLIC INTERVENTION IN AGRICULTURAL INSURANCE QUESTIONNAIRE			
Please read Guidance Notes before completing.			
Respondent's Name			
Respondent's Company		Date	
Country:		Province (if applicable)	
Q. 1 When was agricultural insurance introduced in your country?			
1.1 Crop [Year]		1.2 Livestock [Year]	
1.3 Comments (please add if you wish):			
Q.2 Agricultural Insurance Market Structure in 2007–08			
Please provide a list of the NUMBER of public and private crop and livestock insurance companies active in your country today by CATEGORY.			

Item	Crop Insurance Only	Livestock Insurance Only	Crop + Livestock
Public Sector Insurer(s)			
Private Sector Insurer(s)			
Mutual/Cooperative			
Private Coinsurance Pool			
Public-Private Coinsurance Pool			
Other, specify			
Additional Comments (please add if you wish):			

Q.3 Agricultural Reinsurance Market			
3.1 Are the crop and/or livestock insurance programs reinsured?	Yes ☐		No ☐
If Yes, please specify the type of reinsurance organization for crops and livestock (tick boxes):			
Reinsurance Organization	Crop	Livestock	Types of Reinsurance Support: Quota Share, Stop Loss, Other (specify)
Government			
Public (National) Reinsurer			
Private local Reinsurers			
Private International Reinsurers			
Other, specify			
Additional Comments (please add if you wish):			

3.2 Is access to private international agricultural reinsurance capacity a constraint to the development of crop and livestock insurance products and programs in your country? *(tick appropriate box for each Class/Program)*

Class/Program	No Constraint	Moderate Constraint	Major Constraint
Crop Hail/Named Peril			
Crop MPCI			
Livestock Mortality			
Livestock Epidemic Disease			
Crop Weather Index			
Other, specify			
Additional Comments (Please add if you wish):			

Q.4 Types of Agricultural Insurance Products available through Public and/or Private Insurance Companies in 2007–08 *(Agricultural Insurance market-level question)*		
Item	Public Sector Insurer(s) (tick box)	Private Sector Insurer(s) (tick box)
Indemnity-based Products:		
Crop Hail or named peril		
Crop Multiple Peril (MPCI)		
Crop Income Insurance (Yield + Price protection)		
Crop (Other, specify) MPCI global Portfolio.........		
Crop-Greenhouse		
Forestry		
Livestock Accident and Mortaility		
Livestock Epidemic Disease		
Livestock (Other, specify)..............		
Aquaculture		
Other, specify............................		
Index-based Products		
Weather Index Insurance		
NSVI/RS Index Insurance		
Area-Yield Index Insurance		
Livestock Mortality Insurance		
Other, specify............................		
Additional Comments (please add if you wish):		

Q.5 PUBLIC Sector support to Agricultural Insurance in 2007–08. If NO public sector support to Agricultural or livestock insurance, please pass to Question 6			
5.1 Form of Government Support to Insurers	Crop (Yes/No)	Livestock (Yes/No)	Comments
1. Agricultural Insurance Legislation (Laws)			
2. Start-up Costs for new companies			
3. Insurance Premium subsidies			
4. Subsidies on Insurers' Admin. And Operating Expenses			
5. Subsidies on Loss Assessment Costs			
6. Are government-funded staff involved in loss assessment?			
7. Subsidies on Reinsurance Premiums			
8. Government Reinsurance of Claims			
9. Subsidies for Training and Education			
10. Subsidies for Product Research and Development			
11. Exemption of sales tax on Agric. Insurance Premiums			
12. Other government Support (specify)			

5.2 Who provides public sector agricultural insurance premium subsidies? Provincial governments in some specific cases		
Government Department	Crop Insurance (percent of Total)	Livestock (percent of Total)
Federal Government		
Provincial or Local Government		
Other, specify		
5.3 Premium Subsidies for Crops and Livestock in 2007–08		
Please complete the premium subsidy questions below which apply to your country	Crop	Livestock

5.3.1 Are premium subsidies available for all crops and livestock?	___Yes ___No If NO, which main crops are eligible for premium subsidies (rank in order of importance)	___Yes ___No If NO, which types of livestock are eligible for premium subsidies (rank in order of importance)
	1.............................	1.............................
	2.............................	2.............................
	3.............................	3.............................
	4.............................	4.............................
	5.............................	5.............................
5.3.2 Are all types of crop and livestock producer eligible for premium subsidies?	___Yes ___No If NO, what types of farmers are NOT eligible for premium subsidies?	___Yes ___No If NO, what types of livestock producers are NOT eligible for premium subsidies?
5.3.3 Are small and marginal farmers eligible for special premium subsidies?	___Yes ___No If Yes, details:	___Yes ___No If Yes, details:
5.3.4 Types of premium subsidy and amount		
(a) Premium rates paid by producers capped by government at below actuarial level	___Yes ___No Capped rates as percent of full rates:	___Yes ___No Capped rates as percent of full rates:
(b) Single fixed premium subsidy paid as a percentage of commercial premium rate	___Yes ___No	___Yes ___No
	If Yes, amount of premium paid by Producer as percent of total premium	...... percent	If Yes, amount of premium paid by Producer as percent of total premium	.... percent
	Subsidy amount paid by Government as a percent of total premium	...... percent	Subsidy amount paid by Government as a percent of total premium	.... percent

(c) Variable premium subsidy levels according to crop type or live-stock type and type of producer or region and / or other criteria?	__Yes __No If Yes, please provide details of your variable premium subsidy levels below or attach in Appendix 1.	__Yes __No If Yes, please provide details of your variable premium subsidy levels below or attach in Appendix 1.

Additional Comments (Please add if you wish):

5.4 Costs of Government of Financial Subsidies in last five years

Crop	Please specify Currency		Units		
Year	Insurance Premium Subsidies	Admin. and Operating Expense Subsidies	Loss Adjustment Expense Subsidies	Reinsurance Premium Subsidies	Claims Paid by Govt. Reinsurance

Additional Comments (Please add if you wish):

Livestock	Please Specify Currency		Units		
Year	Insurance Premium Subsidies	Admin. and Operating Expense Subsidies	Loss Adjustment Expense Subsidies	Reinsurance Premium Subsidies	Claims Paid by Govt. Reinsurance

Additional Comments (Please add if you wish):

Total Agricultural Insurance Subsidies (including crop, livestock, aquaculture, forestry, etc.)

Please Specify Currency			Units		
Year	Insurance Premium Subsidies	Admin. and Operating Expense Subsidies	Loss Adjustment Expense Subsidies	Reinsurance Premium Subsidies	Claims Paid by Govt. Reinsurance

Additional Comments (Please add if you wish):

Q.6 Agricultural Insurance Delivery Channels (Note if your response applies to Whole Market or to your Insurance Company only. Please tick applicable box)

____Whole Market ____Insurance Company

6.1 Please specify the main forms of delivery channel for crops and livestock Insurance: Provide ranking in decreasing order of importance (1 = most important)

Channel	Crop	Livestock
Insurer's own agent network		
Insurance Broker		
Banks including Microfinance Organizations		
Producer Associations and Cooperatives		
Inter Suppliers		
Other organization (specify)		

6.2 Do you have any specific Organization(s) delivering agricultural insurance to Small and Marginal farmers?

____Yes ____No

If yes, please explain details:

Q.7 Agricultural Insurance Participation (Adoption) Rates (Note if your response applies to whole market or to your insurance company only, please tick applicable box)

____Whole Market ____Insurance Company

Crop (All Crops)

Year	Number of Crop Policies Issued	Percent of Farmers Purchasing Crop Insurance	Insured Area (Ha)	Percentage of National Crop Area Insured (percent)

Additional Comments: (Please add if you wish)

Livestock (All Livestock as listed)							
Year	Cattle (Number of Insured Animals)	Percent of National Cattle Herd Insured	Swine (Number of Insured Animals)	Percent of National Swine Herd Insured	Sheep and Goats (Number of Insured Animals)	Percent of National Sheep Flock Insured	Poultry (Number of Insured Birds)	Percent of National Poultry Insured

Additional Comments: (Please add if you wish)

Q.8 Agricultural Insurance Results last five years (Note if your response applies to whole market or to your insurance company only, please tick applicable box)

____Whole Market ____Insurance Company

Crop	Please Specify Currency	US$	Units	Tons	
Year	Number of Policies	Total Sum Insured	Premium (inclusive of subsidies)	Paid Claims	Loss Ratio (percent)

Livestock	Please Specify Currency		Units		
Year	Number of Policies	Total Sum Insured	Premium (inclusive of subsidies)	Paid Claims	Loss Ratio (percent)

Total Agricultural Insurance Results (including crop, livestock, aquaculture, forestry, etc)

Please Specify Currency		US$	Units		
Year	Number of Policies	Total Sum Insured	Premium (inclusive of subsidies)	Paid Claims	Loss Ratio (percent)

Q.9 Costs of Agricultural Insurance Provision			
Please provide your best estimates for your insurance company or the agricultural insurance market (tick whichever applied) of the costs of providing crop and livestock insurance in the most recent year available. Please provide your costs expressed as a percentage of the original gross premium rate charged to the farmer			
___Whole Market ____Insurance Company			
Year			
Insurer's costs as a percent of original gross premium			
Item	Crop	Livestock	Other (Specify)............
1. Marketing and Acquisition (commissions)			
2. Insurer's own administration costs <u>excluding</u> in-field loss adjustment costs			
3. Lost adjusting costs			
4. Insurance Premium taxes *(if applicable)*			
Total original gross premium rate (OGP)			
Additional Comments (Please add if you wish):			

	Crop	Livestock
Q.10 Are there other forms of government support to agriculture: including disaster relief or natural catastrophe or epidemic disease compensation for crops and livestock producers?		
10.1 ___Yes ___No If yes, please explain details:		
10.2 Name of Program or Fund		
10.3 Organization(s) responsible for funding		
10.4 Organization(s) responsible for implementation		
10.5 Which perils/event(s) are covered by disaster relief fund?		
10.6 Criteria for declaring a disaster to trigger compensation		
10.7 Is eligibility to disaster relief dependent on buying agricultural insurance		
10.8 Amounts paid by the government in disaster relief to crop and livestock producers by year (Please specify currency..............)		
Additional Comments (Please add if you wish):		

Q. 11 Voluntary versus Compulsory Agricultural Insurance		
Class of Insurance	Voluntary (Yes/No)	If No, Details of Compulsion of Cover (for example, compulsory for crop credit recipients)
Crop		
Livestock		
Additional Comments (Please add if you wish):		

Q.12 If you would like to comment further on the role of public sector intervention in agricultural insurance, please complete the questions below. In your opinion:

a) Is there a NEED for public sector intervention in agricultural insurance in your country? Explain your reasons:

____Yes ___No
Explain your reasons:

b) WHAT is/are the most important form(s) of public sector intervention in agricultural insurance in your country and WHY? Provide up to three forms of intervention, starting with 1 = most important

1) PREMIUM SUBSIDIES..
2) ....
3) ....

c) Are there any drawbacks of public intervention in agricultural insurance in your country?

d) Any other comments you wish to make

Thank you very much for your assistance in participating in this World Bank Survey of Public-Private Agricultural Insurance Provision in your country.
PLEASE RETURN THE COMPLETED QUESTIONNAIRE TO THE COUNTRY COORDINATOR.

APPENDIXES

Please paste any additional information here or send as a separate attach file

Survey Results

This appendix presents the detailed results of the World Bank survey conducted in 2008. Every attempt has been made to present the original figures provided by the survey respondents. Where data reported in the questionnaire were deemed to be inconsistent, the authors have corrected these inconsistencies to the best of their ability. All errors and/or omissions in the analysis of the World Bank survey results are the sole responsibility of the authors.

Table D.1 Countries with and without Subsidies for Crop Insurance, by Income Level

Countries that provide no premium subsidies for crop insurance	Countries that provide premium subsidies for crop insurance	Type of premium subsidy	Fixed subsidy (percent)	Variable subsidy (percent)	Special subsidies for small and marginal farmers
High-income Countries					
	Australia	Fixed	50		Yes
	Canada	Variable		0–100	No
	Cyprus	Fixed	50		No
	Czech Republic	Variable		35–50	
	France	Fixed and variable	35	35–40	Yes
	Israel	Variable	35	35–80	No
	Italy	Fixed	66		No
	Japan	Fixed	50		No
	Portugal	Variable		45–75	No
	Slovenia	Variable		30–50	Yes
	Korea, Rep. of	Fixed	50		No
	Spain	Variable		4–75	No
	Switzerland[b]	Fixed	0		No
	United States	Variable		35–67	No
Upper middle-income Countries					
Argentina[a]	Brazil	Variable		40–60	Yes
Bulgaria	Chile	Fixed	50		Yes
Jamaica	Costa Rica	Variable		40–65	Yes
Panama	Kazakhstan	Variable			
Romania	Mauritius	Fixed	<1		Yes

188

Country	Premium type			Subsidy
South Africa[a]	Variable		35–60	No
Uruguay[a]	Fixed	50		No
Venezuela, R. B. de	Fixed	50		No
Windward Islands	Fixed	50		No
Lower middle-income Countries				
Bolivia, Plurinational State of	Fixed	50		No
China	Variable		30–60	No
Colombia	Variable		33–50	No
Dominican Republic	Fixed	50		Yes
Ecuador	Fixed	70		Yes
Nicaragua	Fixed	50		No
El Salvador	Capped and variable		15–35	Yes
Guatemala	Variable		0–80	No
Honduras	Fixed	80		No
India	Fixed	50		No
Iran, Islamic Rep. of	Variable		30–100	Yes
Moldova	Variable		48–63	No
Morocco	Fixed	50		No
Peru	Fixed	50		No
Low-income Countries				
Ethiopia	Fixed	50		No
Malawi	Fixed	50		No

Source: World Bank Survey 2008.

a Argentina and Uruguay have private crop hail insurance markets that receive no premium subsidies. Both countries have very small subsidized crop insurance programs for specialist crops (vegetables and fruit) in one or two provinces.

b There is no national premium subsidy program in Switzerland, but some cantons provide some financial support on a selected basis.

Table D.2 Extent of Crop and Livestock Insurance Coverage, by Country and Income Level

Country	Number of insured policies	Percentage of farmers insured	National area insured (thousands of hectares)	Percentage of national area insured	Number of heads of cattle insured (thousands)	Percentage of national cattle insured
Countries with No Premium Subsidies						
Australia	25,000	50.0	15,000	50.0	—	5
Germany	—	—	—	—	—	50
Hungary	2,369	—	618	13.4	—	60
New Zealand	1,500	5.0	10	5.0	—	2
Sweden	9,653	—	648	52.0	1,001	> 70 cattle, > 90 pigs and poultry
Switzerland	39,704	70.0	—	75.0	—	—
High-income	—	**41.7**	—	**39.1**	—	—
Argentina	137,079	—	15,958	48.0	—	—
Panama	—	—	1	0.0	—	—
Romania	6,643	—	138	1.5	—	—
South Africa	18,000	25.0	1,500	25.0	—	—
Windward Islands	2,767	63.0	—	62.0	—	—
Upper- middle-income	—	**44.0**	—	**27.3**	—	—
Ecuador	3,228	4.0	27	2.0	<1	—
Mongolia	—	—	—	—	287	1.2
Nicaragua	16	12.0	2	4.9	—	—
Paraguay	300	—	36	1.0	—	—
Thailand	1	—	<1	<0.1	—	—
Lower middle-income	—	**8.0**	—	**2.0**	—	—
Bangladesh	—	—	—	—	<1	—
Ethiopia	3	—	2,462	12.0	<1	<1
Malawi	2,587	1.0	3	2.0	—	—

Nepal	103	0.0	< 1	0.0	10	< 1
Low-Income	—	0.5	—	4.7	—	—
Countries with Premium Subsidies						
Canada	84,221	—	24,755	63.0	—	—
France	69,288	—	3,800	20.5	—	100
Israel	—	85.0	1,340	90.0	220	—
Italy	238,501	—	—	17.4	—	—
Korea, Rep. of	37,849	—	6,774	26.5	—	7 cattle, 67 pigs, 40 poultry
Spain	303,305	91.0	109,951	26.0	1,252	19
United States	1,933,981	88.0	—	90.0	—	—
High-income	—	—	—	47.6	—	< 1
Brazil	31,404	—	2,276	2.6	6	—
Chile	11,120	5.0	69	3.5	—	—
Costa Rica	257	1.0	8	2.0	< 1	—
Kazakhstan	22,908	80.6	11,797	61.2	—	75 swine, 15 cattle, 2 sheep
Mauritius	24,300	100.0	65	100.0	4,352	—
Mexico	54,559	17.0	4,425	21.0	—	—
Poland	15,000	3.0	450	4.0	—	—
Russia	10,143	—	20,200	28.0	56	—
Turkey	207,328	6.9	—	3.0	—	—
Uruguay	—	—	550	68.0	—	—
Venezuela, R. B. de	491	0.5	18	1.0	< 1	—
Upper middle-income	—	26.7	—	26.8	—	—
China	50,000,000	10.0	15,330	10.0	—	—
Colombia	1,566	—	31	1.0	—	—
Dominican Republic	5,292	—	15	2.0	< 1	—
India	20,000,000	15.0	30,000	16.0	8,000	—

(continued)

Table D.2 Extent of Crop and Livestock Insurance Coverage, by Country and Income Level *(continued)*

Country	Number of insured policies	Percentage of farmers insured	National area insured (thousands of hectares)	Percentage of national area insured	Number of heads of cattle insured (thousands)	Percentage of national cattle insured
Iran, Islamic Rep. of	62	34.0	7,327	35.0	645	8
Moldova	145	10.0	73	5.5	—	—
Philippines	37,810	—	70	1.8	4	—
Sudan	130,000	—	278	10.7	3	—
Ukraine	4,397	8.0	2,358	5.0	—	—
Lower middle-income	—	**15.4**	—	**9.7**	—	—

Source: World Bank Survey 2008.

Note: — = Not available.

Table D.3 Premiums, Claims, Subsidies, and Loss Ratios for Crop Insurance, by Country

Country	Period	Total crop premium (millions of dollars)	Total crop claims (millions of dollars)	Loss ratio (percent)	Average crop premium subsidy (percent)	Producer premium (millions of dollars)	Producer loss ratio (percent)
Countries with Crop Premium Subsidies							
Brazil	2004–07	151.2	122.5	81	34	99.9	123
Canada	2003–07	4,272.4	3,158.0	74	52	1,430.7	186
Chile	2003–07	14.0	6.2	45	53	6.6	95
Colombia	2007	5.0	2.4	47	60	2.0	119
Costa Rica	2003–07	1.6	1.4	90	49	0.8	176
Dominican Republic	2003–07	5.0	2.3	46	18	4.1	56
India	2003–07	540.1	1,698.4	314	6	505.3	336
Iran, Islamic Rep. of	2003–07	667.4	1,010.4	151	63	249.3	405
Italy	2003–06	1,269.2	728.9	57	61	494.5	147
Japan	2003–05	1,274.4	1,146.7	90	51	624.8	184
Korea, Rep. of	2003–07	223.6	168.2	74	30	155.7	108
Mexico	2003–07	460.9	200.1	43	40	275.9	73
Philippines	2003–07	9.5	6.9	73	49	4.9	142
Poland	2003–07	17.2	17.4	101	17	14.2	122
Portugal	2003–07	55.4	16.3	29	67	18.4	88
Russian Federation	2003–06	730.7	476.2	65	47	386.3	123
Spain	2003–07	2,091.2	1,744.3	83	66	714.5	244
Sudan	2003–07	13.3	4.5	34	53	6.3	72
United States (MPCI)	2003–07	22,708.1	15,887.1	70	59	9,339.7	170
Countries with No Crop Premium Subsidies							
Argentina	2003–07	706.9	447.2	63		695.0	64
Australia	2003–07	133.2	69.9	52		133.2	52
Bulgaria	2003–05	23.5	17.5	74		23.5	74

(continued)

Table D.3 Premiums, Claims, Subsidies, and Loss Ratios for Crop Insurance, by Country (continued)

Country	Period	Total crop premium (millions of dollars)	Total crop claims (millions of dollars)	Loss ratio (percent)	Average crop premium subsidy (percent)	Producer premium (millions of dollars)	Producer loss ratio (percent)
Czech Republic	2003–05	83.5	42.7	51		83.5	51
Ecuador	2003–07	2.5	1.6	64		2.5	64
Germany	2003–05	463.1	374.3	81		463.1	81
Honduras	2003–07	6.6	4.1	62		6.6	62
Hungary	2003–07	113.6	98.2	86		113.6	86
Malawi	2004–07	0.2	<0.1	1		<0.1	1
Mauritius	2003–07	145.2	100.7	69		145.2	69
Nicaragua	2007–08	0.1	<0.1	36		0.1	36
Panama	2003–07	2.7	2.4	87		2.7	87
Romania	2006–07	0.3	<0.1	21		0.3	21
South Africa	2004–07	43.4	40.3	93		43.4	93
Sweden	2003–07	13.1	5.2	40		13.1	40
Switzerland	2003–07	233.8	269.4	115		233.8	115
United States (crop hail insurance)	2003–07	2,117.2	1,087.2	51		2,117.2	115
Uruguay	2003–07	17.5	6.4	37		17.5	51
Venezuela, R. B. de	2003–07	5.4	4.8	90		5.4	37
Windward Islands	2003–07	3.0	3.6	118		3.0	90

Source: World Bank Survey 2008.

Table D.4 Premiums, Claims, Subsidies, and Loss Ratios for Livestock Insurance, by Country

Country	Period	Total livestock premium (millions of dollars)	Total livestock claims (millions of dollars)	Loss ratio (percent)	Average livestock premium subsidy (percent)	Producer premium (millions of dollars)	Producer loss ratio (percent)
Countries with Livestock Premium Subsidies							
Iran, Islamic Rep. of	2003–07	200.4	1,251.1	624	91	19.0	6601
Italy	2006–07	2.0	0.5	26	49	1.0	51
Japan	2003–05	1,747.6	1,146.7	66	48	903.5	127
Korea, Rep. of	2003–07	148.1	104.0	70	47	78.5	132
Mexico	2003–07	151.0	105.3	70	30	105.0	100
Nepal	2003–06	0.7	0.1	18	50	0.4	36
Poland	2003–07	0.5	0.3	60	1	0.5	61
Spain	2003–07	1,066.8	941.1	88	80	213.4	441
United States (federal livestock)	2003–07	21.6	14.5	67	6	20.2	72
Countries with No Livestock Premium Subsidies							
Argentina	2003–07	0.1	0.04	35		0.1	35
Bulgaria	2003–05	5.8	4.4	75		5.8	75
Colombia	2007	0.1	0.1	12		0.1	12
Costa Rica	2003–07	0.1	0.06	45		0.1	45
Czech Republic	2003–05	51.7	25.8	50		51.7	50
Ecuador	2003–07	1.4	0.9	62		1.4	62
Honduras	2003–07	0.1	0.1	67		0.1	67
Hungary	2003–07	111.0	90.3	81		111.0	81
Mongolia	2006–07	0.2	0.2	115		0.2	115
Panama	2003–07	1.7	0.7	40		1.7	40

(continued)

Table D.4 Premiums, Claims, Subsidies, and Loss Ratios for Livestock Insurance, by Country (continued)

Country	Period	Total livestock premium (millions of dollars)	Total livestock claims (millions of dollars)	Loss ratio (percent)	Average livestock premium subsidy (percent)	Producer premium (millions of dollars)	Producer loss ratio (percent)
Philippines	2003–07	0.3	0.2	57		0.3	57
Romania	2006–07	< 0.1	< 0.1	27		< 0.1	27
Sudan	2003–07	1.4	0.4	31		1.4	31
Sweden	2003–07	41.9	20.0	48		41.9	48
Uruguay	2003–07	12.1	1.7	14		12.1	14

Source: World Bank Survey 2008.

Table D.5 Premiums, Claims, Subsidies, and Loss Ratios for Crop and Livestock Insurance, by Country

Country	Period	Total crop + livestock premium (millions of dollars)	Total crop + livestock claims (millions of dollars)	Loss ratio (percent)	Average total premium subsidy (percent)	Producer premium (millions of dollars)	Producer loss ratio (percent)
Countries with Crop or Livestock Premium Subsidies							
Austria	2003–07	254.9	165.4	65	34	168.9	98
Brazil	2004–07	151.2	122.5	81	34	102.9	119
Canada	2003–07	3,647.4	2,657.1	73	61	1,430.7	186
Chile	2003–07	14.0	6.2	45	53	6.6	95
China	2003–07	983.8	536.5	55	29	701.1	77
Colombia	2007	5.1	2.4	47	60	2.0	116
Costa Rica	2003–07	1.7	1.5	86	45	0.9	158
Czech Republic	2003–05	135.2	68.5	51	n.a.	135.2	51
Dominican Republic	2003–07	5.0	2.3	46	18	4.1	56
India	2003–07	540.1	1,698.4	314	6	505.3	336
Iran, Islamic Rep. of	2003–07	871.2	1,251.1	144	69	271.8	460
Israel	2003–07	122.3	104.1	85	24	93.0	112
Italy	2003–06	1,270.3	728.9	57	61	495.1	147
Japan	2003–05	3,022.0	2,840.7	94	49	1,543.8	184
Korea, Rep. of	2003–07	0.4	0.3	72	37	234.2	116
Malawi	2004–07	0.2	<0.1	1	n.a.	0.2	1
Mexico	2003–07	612.0	305.5	50	38	380.9	80
Moldova	2006–07	3.4	0.8	23	84	0.5	147
Morocco	2003–07	8.3	4.4	53	65	2.9	150
Nepal	2003–06	0.7	0.1	18	50	0.4	36
Nicaragua	2007–08	0.1	<0.1	3	n.a.	0.1	3

(continued)

197

Table D.5 Premiums, Claims, Subsidies, and Loss Ratios for Crop and Livestock Insurance, by Country (continued)

Country	Period	Total crop + livestock premium (millions of dollars)	Total crop + livestock claims (millions of dollars)	Loss ratio (percent)	Average total premium subsidy (percent)	Producer premium (millions of dollars)	Producer loss ratio (percent)
Philippines	2003–07	9.8	7.1	72	47	5.2	137
Poland	2003–07	17.7	17.7	100	17	14.8	120
Portugal	2003–07	55.4	16.3	29	67	18.4	88
Russia	2003–06	730.7	476.2	65	47	386.3	123
Spain	2003–07	3,171.7	2,696.1	85	71	918.3	294
Sudan	2003–07	14.8	5.0	34	48	7.7	64
United States (federal program)	2003–07	22,729.7	15,901.6	70	59	9,414.3	169
Countries with No Crop or Livestock Premium Subsidies							
Argentina	2003–07	707.0	447.3	63	n.a.	695.1	64
Australia[a]	2003–07	133.2	69.9	52	n.a.	133.2	52
Bulgaria	2003–05	29.3	14.9	51	n.a.	29.3	51
Ecuador	2003–07	3.9	2.5	63	n.a.	3.9	63

Germany	2003–05	463.1	374.3	81	n.a.	463.1	81
Honduras	2003–07	6.7	4.1	62	n.a.	6.7	62
Hungary	2003–07	224.6	188.4	84	n.a.	224.6	84
Mauritius	2003–07	145.2	100.7	69	n.a.	145.2	69
Mongolia	2006–07	0.2	0.2	115	n.a.	0.2	115
Panama	2003–07	4.5	3.1	68	n.a.	4.5	68
Romania	2006–07	0.3	0.06	21	n.a.	0.3	21
Slovenia	2003–05	41.7	19.5	47	n.a.	41.1	47
South Africa[a]	2004–07	43.4	40.3	93	n.a.	43.4	93
Sweden	2003–07	54.9	25.3	46	n.a.	54.9	46
Switzerland[a]	2003–07	233.8	269.4	115.2	n.a.	233.8	115
United States (crop hail insurance)	2003–07	2,117.2	1,087.2	51	n.a.	2,117.2	51
Uruguay	2003–07	29.6	8.1	27	n.a.	29.6	27
Venezuela, R. B. de	2003–07	5.4	4.8	90	n.a.	5.4	90
Windward Islands	2003–07	3.0	3.6	118	n.a.	3.0	118

Source: World Bank Survey 2008.

Note: n.a. = Not applicable.

[a] Country has livestock insurance, but survey provided information only on crop insurance.

Table D.6 Average Crop and Livestock Insurance Premium Rates, by Country, 2003–07

Country	Period	Type of crop insurance	Crop	Livestock	All agriculture
Countries with Premium Subsidies					
Brazil	2004–07	MPCI, named peril	4.8	2.5	4.6
Canada	2003–07	MPCI	10.3	—	—
China	2003–07	MPCI, named peril	4.3	5.3	6.6
Colombia	2007	MPCI	5.6	5.0	5.6
Costa Rica	2003–07	MPCI	6.3	—	—
Dominican Republic	2003–07	MPCI	6.4	—	—
Italy	2003–06	MPCI, named peril	7.6	0.4	7.5
India	2003–07	MPCI	3.0	—	—
Israel	2003–07	MPCI	—	—	1.6
Japan	2003–05	MPCI	3.5	4.8	4.1
Korea, Rep. of	2003–07	MPCI, named peril	7.8	7.1	7.5
Mexico	2003–07	MPCI, named peril	7.7	1.6	4.0
Nepal	2003–06	—	—	8.1	—
Philippines	2003–07	MPCI	11.6	4.5	11.0
Portugal	2003–07	MPCI (no drought)	6.7	—	—
Russia	2003–06	MPCI	6.6	—	—
Spain	2003–07	MPCI, named peril	5.7	4.8	6.6
Sudan	2003–07	MPCI	7.2	10.3	7.4
United States (government-subsidized Federal Crop Insurance Program)	2003–07	MPCI	9.1	3.2	9.1
Average premium rates	2003–07	n.a.	6.7	4.5	6.3

Countries with No Premium Subsidies

Country	Period	Type			
Argentina	2003–07	Named peril	5.0	3.3	5.0
Austria	2003–05	Named peril	—	—	2.5
Bulgaria	2003–05	Named peril	4.8	0.9	3.8
Ecuador	2003–07	MPCI	3.7	6.5	4.4
Germany	2003–05	Named peril	1.1	—	—
Malawi	2004–07	Weather index	5.5	—	—
Mauritius	2003–07	Named peril (catastrophe)	8.2	—	—
Mongolia	2006–07	n.a.	—	1.7	—
Nicaragua	2007–08	Weather index	5.4	—	—
Panama	2003–07	MPCI	4.9	3.9	4.5
Romania	2006–07	Named peril	2.1	4.3	2.1
South Africa	2004–07	MPCI, named peril	4.5	—	—
United States (private crop hail)	2003–07	Named peril	2.8	—	—
Uruguay	2003–07	MPCI, named peril	3.9	0.3	0.7
Venezuela, R. B. de	2003–07	MPCI	6.1	—	—
Windward Islands	2003–07	Named peril (catastrophe)	11.7	—	—
Average premium rates	2003–07	n.a.	5.0	3.0	3.4

Source: World Bank Survey 2008.
Note: — = Not available. n.a. = Not applicable.

Table D.7 U.S. Federal Crop Insurance Program Operating Results, 2003–07 (millions of dollars, except where otherwise indicated)

Item	2003	2004	2005	2006	2007	2008	2003–07	1981–2008
Indemnity	3,260	3,210	2,367	3,504	3,546	8,634	15,887	53,583
Total premium[a]	3,431	4,186	3,949	4,579	6,562	9,852	22,708	58,291
Premium subsidy	2,042	2,477	2,344	2,682	3,823	5,691	13,368	31,003
Producer premium	1,389	1,709	1,605	1,897	2,739	4,161	9,340	27,288
Net indemnity	1,871	1,501	762	1,606	808	4,474	6,548	26,295
A&O expense subsidies	734	888	829	962	1,335	2,004	4,748	—
Special reinsurance agreement net underwriting gain	378	692	915	819	1,569	1,119	4,373	—
Total delivery costs[b]	1,112	1,580	1,744	1,781	2,904	3,123	9,121	20,453
Total insurance outlays	2,982	3,081	2,506	3,387	3,712	7,596	15,668	46,749
Loss ratio (indemnity/total premium) (percent)	95	77	60	77	54	88	70	92
Producer loss ratio (indemnity/total premium) (percent)	235	188	147	185	129	208	170	196
Hazell ratio (indemnity + total delivery costs)/producer premium) (percent)	315	280	256	279	236	283	389	208
Transfer efficiency (net indemnities/total insurance outlays) (percent)	63	49	30	47	22	59	42	56
A&O expense ratio (percent)	21	21	21	21	20	20	21	—

Source: Glauber 2007 for figures through 2005; Glauber and Skees (personal communication) for 2006–08.

Note: — = Not available.

a Under the U.S. Federal Crop Insurance Program, the total premium comprises premium subsidies and premiums paid by the producer. It is equivalent to the net rather than the original gross premium, because it excludes A&O expense and profit allocations.

b Total delivery costs include A&O expenses and reinsurance payments (net underwriting gain or loss) made by the government under the special reinsurance agreement.

References

Air Worldwide. 2009. *Agricultural Risk and the Crop Insurance Market in China.* Boston.

Anderson, J. 2001. "Risk Management in Rural Development: A Review." Rural Strategy Background Paper 7, World Bank, Washington, DC.

Babcock, B. A., and D. A. Hennessy. 1996. "Input Demand under Yield and Revenue Insurance." *American Journal of Agricultural Economics* 78 (May): 416–27.

Barnett, B. J., C. B. Barrett, and J. R. Skees. 2007. "Poverty Traps and Index-Based Risk Transfer Products." *World Development* 36 (10): 1766–85.

Bekkerman, A., B. K. Goodwin, and N. E. Piggott. 2008. "Spatio-temporal Risk and Severity Analysis of Soybean Rust in the United States." *Journal of Agricultural and Resource Economics* 33 (3): 311–31.

Binswanger, H. P. 1980. "Attitude toward Risk: Experimental Measurement in Rural India." *American Journal of Agricultural Economics* 62 (3): 375–407.

Breusted, G., and D. Larson. 2006. "Mutual Crop Insurance and Moral Hazard: The Case of Mexican Fondos." Paper presented at the annual meeting of the International Association of Agricultural Economists.

Carpenter, G. 2006. *Global Agriculture Insurance and Reinsurance Market Overview.* Guy Carpenter and Co: New York.

Coate, S. 1995. "Altruism, the Samaritan's Dilemma, and Government Policy Transfer." *American Economic Journal* 85 (1): 46–57.

Cummins J. D., and O. Mahul. 2009. *Catastrophe Risk Financing in Developing Countries: Principles for Public Intervention.* Washington, DC: World Bank.

De Janvry, A., M. Fafchamps, and E. Sadoulet. 1991. "Peasant Household Behavior with Missing Markets: Some Paradoxes Explained." *Economic Journal* 101 (409): 1400–07.

European Commission. 2001. *Risk Management Tools for EU Agriculture with a Special Focus on Insurance.* January. http://ec.europa.eu/agriculture/publi/insurance/index_en.htm.

———. 2006. *Agricultural Insurance Schemes.* December, modified February 2008. http://ec.europa.eu/agriculture/analysis/external/insurance/index_en.htm.

FAO (Food and Agriculture Organization). 1991a. *Crop Insurance Compendium,* ed. P. L. Cottle. Agricultural Services Division, Marketing and Credit Service, Rome.

———. 1991b. *Strategies for Crop Insurance Planning,* ed. R. A. J. Roberts and W. J. A. Dick. FAO Agricultural Services Bulletin 86, Rome.

Glauber, J. 2007. *Double Indemnity: Crop Insurance and the Failure of U.S. Agricultural Disaster Policy.* AEI Agricultural Policy Series: The 2007 Farm Bill and Beyond. American Enterprise Institute, Washington, DC. http://www.aei.org/docLib/20070515_glauberfinal.pdf.

———. 2001. "Problems with Market Insurance in Agriculture." *American Journal of Agricultural Economics* 83 (3): 643–49.

Goodwin, B. K., and V. H. Smith. 1995. *The Economics of Crop Insurance and Disaster Aid.* Washington, DC: AEI Press.

Gurenko, E., and O. Mahul. 2004. "Enabling Productive but Asset-Poor Farmers to Succeed: A Risk Financing Framework." World Bank Policy Research Working Paper 3211, Washington, DC.

Hazell, P. B. R. 1992. "The Appropriate Role of Agricultural Insurance in Lower Income Countries." *Journal of International Development* 4 (6): 567–81.

Hazell, P. B. R., C. Pomareda, and A. Valdes. 1986. *Crop Insurance for Agricultural Development.* Baltimore, MD: Johns Hopkins University Press.

Holzmann, R., and S. Jorgensen. 2000. *Social Risk Management: A New Conceptual Framework for Social Protection and Beyond.* Social Protection Discussion Paper 6, World Bank, Washington, DC.

Horowitz, J. K., and E. Lichtenberg. 1993. "Insurance, Moral Hazard, and Chemical Use in Agriculture." *American Journal of Agricultural Economics* 75 (4): 926–35.

IPCC (Intergovernmental Panel for Climate Change). 2007. *IPCC Fourth Assessment Report.* Geneva.

James, P. C., and R. Nair. 2009. *A Study of Yield-Based Crop Insurance in India: A Performance Review.* Agricultural Insurance Company of India: New Delhi.

Kasten, E. 2005. "Eyes in the Sky Aid Crop Insurers." ICMIF Global Issue 51. http://www.eomd.esa.int/files/contracts/131-176-149-30_200521014421.pdf.

Kramer, R. A. 1983. "Federal Crop Insurance: 1938–82." *Agricultural History* 57 (2): 181–200.

Kunreuther, H. 1976. "Limited Knowledge and Insurance Protection." *Public Policy* 24 (2): 227–61.

Mahul, O. 2005. "The Financing of Agricultural Production Risks: Revisiting the Role of Agricultural Insurance." GCMNB World Bank, Washington, DC.

Mahul, O., and J. R. Skees. 2007. "Managing Agricultural Risk at the Country Level: The Case of Index-Based Livestock Insurance in Mongolia." World Bank Policy Research Working Paper 4325, Washington, DC.

Mahul, O., D. Clarke, and N. Verma. 2009. "Weather-Based Crop Insurance for Indian Farmers: Suggested Revised Ratemaking Methodology." SASFP and GCMNB World Bank, Washington, DC.

Mapfre. 1984. *Crop Insurance in the Countries of the Third World*. Report of the Fourth Third World Insurance Congress, Casablanca. Corporacion Mapfre S.A., Madrid.

———. 1986. *Crop Insurance Experience in the World*. Report of the Fifth Third World Insurance Congress, Beijing. Corporacion Mapfre S.A., Madrid.

Miranda, M. J., and J. W. Glauber. 1997. "Systemic Risk, Reinsurance, and the Failure of Crop Insurance Markets." *American Journal of Agricultural Economics* 79 (1): 206–15.

Moscardi, E., and A. de Janvry. 1977. "Attitude toward Risk among Peasants: An Econometric Approach." *American Journal of Agricultural Economics* 59 (November): 710–16.

Paris Re. 2008. "Agricultural Insurance Market." Paper presented at the annual meeting of the International Task Force, Brusssels, October 22–24.

Roth, J., M. McCord, and D. Liber. 2007. "The Landscape of Microinsurance in the World's 100 Poorest Countries." MicroInsurance Centre.

Seo, J., and O. Mahul. 2009. "The Impact of Climate Change on Catastrophe Risk Model: Implication for Catastrophe Risk Markets in Developing Countries." World Bank Policy Research Working Paper 4959, Washington, DC.

Siamwalla, A., and A. Valdes. 1986. "Should Crop Insurance be Subsidized?" In *Crop Insurance for Agricultural Development*, ed. P. B. R. Hazell, C. Pomareda, and A. Valdes. Baltimore MD: Johns Hopkins University Press.

Skurai, T., and T. Reardon. 1997. "Potential Demand for Drought Insurance in Burkina Faso and its Determinants." *American Journal of Agricultural Economics* 79 (4): 1193–1207.

Smith, V. H., and B. K. Goodwin, 1996. "Crop Insurance, Moral Hazard, and Agricultural Chemical Use." *American Journal of Agricultural Economics* 78 (May): 428–38.

Swiss Re. 2007. *Insurance in Emerging Markets*. Sigma 01/2007, Zurich.

UNCTAD (United Nations Conference on Trade and Development). 1994. *Agricultural Insurance in Developing Countries.* UNCTAD/SDD/INS/1/Rev 1, 8 June, Geneva.

Varangis, P., D. J. Larson, and J. Anderson. 2002. "Agricultural Markets and Risks: Management of the Latter, Not the Former." World Bank Policy Research Working Paper 2793, Washington, DC.

World Bank. 2005. *Managing Agricultural Production Risks: Innovations in Developing Countries.* Report 32727, Agriculture and Rural Development Department, Washington, DC.

———. 2006. *Overcoming Drought: Adaptation Strategies for Andhra Pradesh, India.* Washington, DC.

———. 2007a. *China: Innovations in Agricultural Insurance: Promoting Access to Agricultural Insurance for Small Farmers.* East Asia Agricultural and Rural Development Department and Finance and Private Sector Unit, Washington, DC.

———. 2007b. *India: National Agricultural Insurance Scheme: Market-Based Solutions for Better Risk Sharing.* Report 39353, South Asia Finance and Private Sector Unit, Washington, DC.

———. 2008. *World Development Report 2008: Agriculture for Development.* Washington, DC: World Bank.

Wright, B. D., and J. A. Hewitt. 1994. "All Risk Crop Insurance: Lessons from Theory and Practice." In *Economics of Agricultural Crop Insurance: Theory and Evidence,* ed. Darell L. Hueth and W. Hartley Furtan. Boston: Kluwer.

Index

Figures, notes, and tables are indicated by *f, n,* and *t,* respectively.

ECO-AUDIT
Environmental Benefits Statement

The World Bank is committed to preserving endangered forests and natural resources. The Office of the Publisher has chosen to print *Government Support to Agricultural Insurance* on recycled paper with 30 percent postconsumer fiber in accordance with the recommended standards for paper usage set by the Green Press Initiative, a nonprofit program supporting publishers in using fiber that is not sourced from endangered forests. For more information, visit www.greenpressinitiative.org.

Saved:
- 5 trees
- 2 million BTU's of total energy
- 498 lbs of CO_2 equivalent of greenhouse gases
- 2,399 gallons of wastewater
- 146 pounds of solid waste